BAUDELAIRE AS A LOVE POET

Peint et Gravé par Manet 1862.   Imp. A. Salmon.

*Commemorating the Centenary of the
Death of the Poet*

BAUDELAIRE
AS A LOVE POET
AND OTHER ESSAYS

Edited by LOIS BOE HYSLOP

Essays by
HENRI PEYRE
RENÉ GALAND
MARCEL RUFF
LOIS BOE HYSLOP
&
FRANCIS E. HYSLOP

1969
*THE PENNSYLVANIA STATE
UNIVERSITY PRESS*
University Park & London

To

JOHN M. ANDERSON

Director of the Institute for the Arts and the

Humanistic Studies

who contributed so greatly to the

organization of the Baudelaire Symposium

and to the publication of

this volume

FOREWORD

"Nous devrions pourtant lui porter quelques fleurs"

Although it was of Mariette, his old childhood servant—"la servante au grand coeur"—that Baudelaire wrote these moving words, they seem especially applicable to the poet himself on the hundredth anniversary of his death.

On August 31, 1867, in a nursing home in the Quartier de Chaillot in Paris, Charles Baudelaire died peacefully in the arms of his mother. For more than a year he had remained speechless and half paralyzed after the stroke which he had suffered while still in Belgium, where he had gone in a last desperate effort to find a publisher for his collected works.

During the first months of his long illness, Baudelaire seemed not without hope of recovery, and his expressive eyes reflected the interest that he took in the conversation of those who came to see him. At first he would even occasionally accompany a small group of intimate friends to lunch and listen in helpless silence as they talked, his frustration at remaining speechless clearly revealed by his burning eyes and his repetition of the only word he could pronounce—*crénom, crénom*.

But as the long months passed without any indication of improvement, Baudelaire seemed to lose all will to live. His strength gradually ebbed and he no longer left his bed. His ravaged features and prematurely white hair made him appear far older than his forty-six years and testified to the torment he had suffered during those last years of disease, loneliness, and despair.

A few loyal friends remained faithful to the end, among them Nadar, Manet, Asselineau, and Banville. Remembering his love of music and particularly his enthusiasm for Wagner, the wives of Paul Meurice and Édouard Manet came to play selections for him from the composer whom he had so brilliantly defended before an indifferent public.

Ironically enough, Baudelaire died the very day that the *Revue Nationale* began the publication of the last series of his *Petits Poèmes en Prose*. But the general public, to whom the poet was more or less unknown, paid little attention and seemed completely oblivious of the fact that France had lost one of its greatest writers. Even Mme Aupick, who had loved her son without ever really understanding him, had only just become aware of his importance, influenced, no doubt, by the few friends and men of letters who had long recognized his strange and original genius.

On September 2, 1867, Baudelaire's funeral was held in the Eglise Saint-Honoré in Passy. About one hundred people attended the service and, of these, not more than sixty followed the coffin to the cemetery of Montparnasse, where the poet was laid to rest beside the grave of his stepfather, General Aupick.

Neither Sainte-Beuve nor Gautier were present at the funeral. The famous critic who, for reasons of health, had declined to pronounce the funeral oration, seemed to have failed

Baudelaire in death as he had failed him in life. Gautier, who was well known for his horror of death and for his avoidance of funerals, was in Geneva and in a letter to his daughter voiced no expression of grief at the death of the friend and admirer who had done more to honor his genius than any other person of his day. The Societé des gens de lettres failed to send the customary representative, in spite of Asselineau's request.

Théodore de Banville and Charles Asselineau spoke movingly at the grave, hoping to accord Baudelaire the recognition in death that had been denied him in life. Banville, who had known Baudelaire since his days at the Hôtel Pimodan, was almost ill with grief and fatigue. Fighting to hold back his tears, he hailed the author of *Les Fleurs du Mal* as a writer of "genius" whose poetry would take its place in literature as "essentially French, essentially original, and essentially new."

Banville was followed in turn by Asselineau who, in a voice choked with emotion, sought to dispel the ugly legends which had grown up around Baudelaire's name and which had completely obscured the real man. Those who did not know the author of *Les Fleurs du Mal,* he maintained, had accepted the legends at face value, failing to understand that the poet's "ironic reserve" was only "a supreme form of dignity"—a mask that he had adopted in an effort to hide the sensitive inner man from the hostile world about him.

But while Asselineau was still speaking, the rain that had been threatening all day began to fall, and those who had braved the oppressive heat and the darkening skies quickly and silently dispersed.

In the last unhappy years before Baudelaire's death there were growing indications that his genius was being slowly recognized among the writers of the younger generation, most of whom were still comparatively unknown. In England, as early as 1862, Swinburne had written a highly laudatory article about *Les Fleurs du Mal* which he published on September 6 of that year in *The Spectator*. In France, Catulle Mendès, Villiers de l'Isle Adam, and Léon Cladel were enthusiastic in their praise of Baudelaire's poetic genius.

In 1865, shortly before Baudelaire became seriously ill in Brussels, Paul Verlaine, who was then a young, unknown writer, published a series of three articles in *L'Art* (November 16 and 30, December 23) in which he acclaimed the originality and the strange power of the author of *Les Fleurs du Mal*. Writing to Baudelaire in Brussels, Sainte-Beuve told him: "You have been very well treated in a newly established journal, *L'Art*. . . . If you were here, you would become, whether or not you wished it, an authority, an oracle, a consulting poet."

But except for a few voices raised in his defense, Baudelaire remained largely neglected and forgotten, unable to find an editor for his collected works and fearful that he might never again succeed in publishing what he had written. On November 13, 1865 he wrote to his friend Hippolyte Le Josne: "I see in the windows of every bookstore all sorts of stupid and useless things and I wonder what keeps me from selling five or six creditable volumes. From time to time, I conclude *very seriously that I shall never again be able to have anything of mine printed, and that I shall never again see my mother or my friends."*

Baudelaire's fears were far from being groundless. After all, in 1864 the editor of the *Figaro* had decided to discontinue the publication of a number of his prose poems "simply because my poems bored everyone," as Baudelaire wrote his mother on the third of March.

Baudelaire's death was the signal for the appearance of a spate of necrological articles in which journalists and critics seemed to vie with each other in relating preposterous anecdotes, most of them without any foundation in fact. In their book, *Baudelaire devant ses contemporains,* W. T. Bandy and Claude Pichois have revealed the degree to which even serious writers went in detailing the perversity, the sadism, and the diabolic tendencies of the dead poet. For many of them, *Les Fleurs du Mal* was still only the poetry of the charnel house and Baudelaire himself an evil figure associated with Satanism and Black Masses.

Knowing full well that the press would hardly forgo the opportunity of appealing to the morbid curiosity of a narrow-minded public, Nadar wrote to the editor of the *Figaro* asking to be allowed to write the obituary of his friend: "Many stupid things will now be said about this very gifted and honorable man which will deeply hurt and anger those who loved and respected him. If you want the *truth* about him in your paper, I am prepared to give it to you."

Nadar's request was granted and, though his article may not have succeeded in convincing the public, it brought great comfort to the poet's friends and above all to his mother, who was delighted and obviously relieved by Nadar's conviction that her son had died a believer.

Nadar's effort to rehabilitate Baudelaire was followed by Gautier's preface to Lévy's complete edition of the author's works, which began to appear in 1868, and by Asselineau's perceptive biographical and critical study, *Charles Baudelaire, sa vie et ses œuvres,* published in 1869. After 1869, the genius of the author of *Les Fleurs du Mal* could no longer be denied, though it was still not unanimously acknowledged until some fifty years later.

In the hundred years that have passed since his death, the cult of Baudelaire has continued to grow until he has become the object of universal admiration, known not only for his magnificent poetry, but also for his translations of Poe and for his remarkable literary and art criticism. *Les Fleurs du Mal* has been translated into many languages, including Russian and Japanese, and, whether we regard that volume of verse as a fundamental source of modern poetry, with Crépet and Blin, or as a splendid culmination, with Henri Peyre, it is clear that it is of central importance in the history of French poetry.

As a critic of his contemporaries, Baudelaire's perspicacity and judgment surpasses that of his great colleague, Sainte-Beuve. In the field of literature, his critical essays on *Madame Bovary,* on Hugo's *La Légende des Siècles,* and on the poetry of Gautier and Leconte de Lisle show remarkable insight and penetration. In art, he was among the first to recognize the genius of Delacroix, Manet, Meryon, Daumier, and Whistler. In music, he was among the first to defend publicly the music of Wagner and to write a brilliant essay on his behalf.

Even more interesting and provocative than his criticism of specific artists are the ideas on aesthetics which he developed in the course of his essays and which are still pertinent to an understanding and appreciation of modern art in general.

Finally, as a translator Baudelaire's rendering of Edgar Allan Poe's five volumes of tales, together with the three essays in which he defended Poe's genius, explain to a large degree the tremendous popularity that the American writer still enjoys in France as well as in other countries of the non-English speaking world.

The hundredth anniversary of Baudelaire's death was designated *L'Année Baudelaire* by André Malraux, Minister of

State in Charge of Cultural Affairs, and the poet's memory was honored both in France and elsewhere by a flurry of literary activity which has continued well into 1968. Several periodicals devoted entire issues to the poet, among them *Revue d'histoire littéraire de la France, Revue des sciences humaines, La Table Ronde,* and *Europe.*

Among the books on Baudelaire published in 1967 should be mentioned *Baudelaire* by Pierre Emmanuel; *Baudelaire: Enfer ou ciel, qu'importe!* by Max Milner; and *Lettres inédites aux siens,* a volume of unpublished Baudelaire letters edited by Philippe Auserve. Of somewhat unusual interest was the album prepared by Claude Pichois, *Baudelaire à Paris,* containing one hundred and twenty-two illustrations including numerous original photographs by Maurice Rué. The year 1967 also marked the appearance of the final volume of the *Œuvres complètes de Charles Baudelaire* edited by Yves Florenne, as well as the reprint of Jean Pommier's distinguished study, *La Mystique de Baudelaire.*

In addition to the many books and articles devoted to Baudelaire, several symposia were held to honor the poet's memory and to provide scholars with an opportunity for fruitful discussion. In France, the distinguished Baudelaire scholar, Marcel Ruff, organized a colloquium held at the Université de Nice where he is Dean of the Faculté des Lettres and des Sciences Humaines. In England, Lloyd James Austin of Cambridge University, the author of *L'Univers poétique de Baudelaire,* organized a symposium held at the Institut Français in London.

In the United States, a symposium organized by Lois Boe Hyslop was held on November 4, 1967, on the campus of The Pennsylvania State University in University Park. This volume is the permanent record of the material presented there. The Pennsylvania State University Press, aided by a generous grant from the Institute for the Arts and the Humanistic Studies, has undertaken to publish these papers in the present commemorative volume.

I should like to take this opportunity to express my sincere appreciation to all those who helped to make the Baudelaire Symposium possible. I am especially grateful to John M. Anderson, Director of the Institute for the Arts and the Humanistic Studies, to Cyril F. Hager, Associate Dean for Continuing Education, and to Edouard Morot-Sir, Director of The Cultural Services of the French Embassy in New York, for their generous financial support. I should also like to thank the departments of Art History, of Philosophy, and of Spanish, Italian, and Portuguese for their active support and at the same time to acknowledge the helpful suggestions of William T. Bandy, Professor of French and Director of the newly established Center for Baudelaire Studies at Vanderbilt University.

And finally, I wish to express my deep gratitude to Gérard J. Brault, Head of the Department of French, for his enthusiastic cooperation and his valuable assistance.

Lois Boe Hyslop

University Park

CONTENTS

BAUDELAIRE AS A LOVE POET
AND OTHER ESSAYS

*Commemorating the Centenary of
the Death of the Poet*

BAUDELAIRE AS A LOVE POET

HENRI PEYRE

It is the fate of professors and critics that they are frequently induced, or constrained, to dissert on that eternal theme of most literatures: love, as beautified or maligned by poets and novelists. They may not be the most competent persons to attempt it, being more familiar with books than with the play of emotions and the display of passions. Daring is not normally what is required of those who watch over the traditions inherited from the past or who scrutinize with a frown the productions of their contemporaries. Yeats, who mocked "the scholars" in an ironical little piece thus entitled, wrote elsewhere:

> What do they know of love, who do not know,
> He keeps his nest upon a windy ledge,
> Above a precipice?

However, if the vicarious experience of life through literature ever serves a purpose, it is where the motif of love is concerned. The epigrammatic remark of La Rochefoucauld holds true, that most people would never fall in love (or not in the manner in which they do), if they had not previously heard and read about it. In no realm of life, probably, are the very young, and even the not so young, prone to behave and even to feel as they have watched characters in fiction or on the screen do. Poetry about death, or about glory, or about wine (except for a very few Horatian and medieval invitations to enjoy man's privilege of drinking without thirst), even poetry about nature in springtime or on the message lent to birds' songs, is seldom recited aloud by average cultured individuals. Lyrics, madrigals, odes about love or women will readily come to the lips of adolescents discovering the thrilling complexities of what is called the heart. It is said that, less naively, a number of men who have left their adolescence behind them have, through expert quoting or borrowing of poetry, appealed to the imagination, to the conceit, or to the senses of younger women. Feminine strategy of seduction has not as a rule needed the help of literature to the same extent.

French literature, except in the age of the troubadours and of Tristan and Isolde, has not been the richest in love poetry. Italy pursued and refined the Troubadour tradition more steadily than has France, from the "Dolce stil nuovo" to the followers of Petrarch. England, which continental Europeans hardly used to regard as a land of exemplary lovers, may well boast of the most varied love poetry ever composed, from Wyatt and Surrey through Sidney, Donne, even some playful eighteenth-century verse, to Shelley, Browning, Yeats, Auden. Except for Du Bellay and Lamartine, Platonism as a source of poetic inspiration inspired very few of the bards of a country in other respects prone to stressing intellectual and cerebral values. If ranks could ever be assigned in such matters, it is likely that, even before Ronsard and Eluard, his closest competitors, Baudelaire would be crowned by most twentieth-century readers as the greatest of love poets in the French language. Musset, once the favorite singer of the woes of loving, recited in state at the Comédie Française for the edification of the young, is far from contemptible, in spite of the scorn poured over his "Nuits" by Baudelaire himself and by Rimbaud. Two philosophers at least, Taine and Bergson, viewed him as their favorite poet; and his comedies have analyzed and dramatized the conflicts of the heart more felicitously than any in France since Marivaux. Still, compared to Baudelaire, he often sounds declamatory and hollow. Victor Hugo lived for love more and longer than any other French poet. His letters to his bride, when he was not yet twenty, have an exquisite delicacy. He blended the thrill of panic terror and that of sensual desire powerfully in "Crépuscule" and in other poems on nature lavishing invitations to sensual union. But, all too often, he was overwhelmed by the consciousness of his own godhead; he then wrote on love as an Olympian honoring mortal women with his own fastuous tributes and with his prodigal, and none too discriminating, embraces.

The originality of Baudelaire's love poetry was not perceived at once by his contemporaries. It is strange indeed to realize how seldom he was imitated in the nineteenth and even in the twentieth centuries. In their very early poems, Verlaine and Mallarmé attempted some effects of rhythm and of imagery reminiscent of the *Fleurs du Mal,* but they soon discovered that their own vocation lay elsewhere: in fact, in attempting the very innovations which Baudelaire would have rejected, in manipulating syntax (Mallarmé) and in experimenting with popular language, with a plebeian and roguish manner of speech, and in dethroning the Alexandrine verse from its hallowed sovereignty (Verlaine). Few clichés in criticism are so shallow and baseless as the one which takes it for granted that Baudelaire is the fountainhead of modern French poetry. Rather than a beginning, he is an end: the supreme flowering of romanticism, with even more fondness for abstract and general words, for comparisons preferred to images, for the universalization of the particular, than had been evinced by the French romantics clinging to their ineradicable classicism. The Symbolists very seldom imitated him. They were strikingly cool to him, either maintaining an eloquent silence (Mallarmé, Verlaine, Henri de Régnier) or multiplying reservations on his greatness (Laforgue, Gourmont, later Apollinaire and Valéry). The one twentieth-century poet whose affinities were with the dolorous strains of the *Fleurs du Mal* was Pierre Reverdy, and he almost excluded the theme of love from his poetry. The whole poetics, and also the achievement, of Paul Valéry were away from Baudelaire, and in his *Notebooks* he vented his animadversion toward him almost as insistently as he did against Pascal. No Frenchman, in verse, invoked Baudelaire as movingly as had Swinburne in his "Ave atque Vale":

O sleepless heart and sombre soul unsleeping . . .

In the realm of love poetry, Verlaine, Apollinaire, and Eluard are the only ones, since *Les Fleurs du Mal,* to have struck an original note and to have restored to that theme the musical hauntingness which has caused their shorter lyrics to be recited and sung by large numbers of people, in a culture where "Lieder" or lyrics have seldom reached the masses. Mallarmé, at the age of twenty-three and two years before the death of Baudelaire, had decided to expel the love theme from his poetry. He wrote to his friend Lefébure in February 1865:

Love is far too much the aim of your poems, and that most colorless word often recurs in them in a rather insipid manner. Unless it be set off by a strange condiment, lust, ecstasy, disease, asceticism, that indefinite feeling does not seem to me to be poetical. As for me, I could, in verse, only utter that word with a smile. . . . Love, if simple, is much too natural a feeling to give a sensation to the blasé poets who read verse. . . . What chiefly turned me against that word, which I only pronounce or write with a certain unpleasant impression, is the foolishness with which five or six jokers among poets have set themselves up as the priests of that big boy, ruddy and chubby like a butcher's son, whom they call Eros, watching themselves with the ecstasy of martyrdom whenever they perform its facile rites, and climb over the women whom they had seduced as on funeral pyres. . . .

Paul Valéry was not yet twenty-five when, in the flush of his Mallarmean admiration, he likewise counseled his friend Pierre Louÿs to eschew the theme of love in poetry: "Love is disappearing. . . . Only some stupid fools will still make it the chief theme of the world. Romeo and Juliet bore me prodigiously. We have at last learned how to make the sauce without those deplorable fish."

The subject is indeed fraught with perils, not the least of which are artificial exaltation, strings of litanies to dull the coyness or the clearsightedness of the woman to be seduced poetically, literary devices used to spread the contagion of desire, working on the senses through the arousing of imagination, promises of bestowing unheard of pleasures or guarantees of immortality proffered in mendacious verse. Worse still, monotony is the bane of those would-be erotic catalogues of the hair, eyes, cheeks, lips, and so on of the lady, painstakingly reaching the ankles and the shoes and concluding that her walk truly reveals the goddess in her. If the tradition commands that the soul be praised rather than the body, that love and death be invoked as twin brothers, or that the firm welding of the lovers be only achieved amid Elysian groves and by creatures having shuffled off this mortal coil and abdicated desire, love poetry can become even more trite and sickening. Baudelaire has not altogether eschewed all those pitfalls of Petrarchian, Sadistic, or Platonic banality. He lapsed into others, partly on account of the relative poverty, or excessive restraint, of his vocabulary. His use of adjectives is often awkward and some of his comparisons trite: "Et ton esprit n'est pas un gouffre moins amer" or "Des plaisirs plus aigus que la glace ou le fer." There are too many vampires in his verse; the sting of kisses or that of remorse are too easily likened to venom and woman to a viper. Her body is conventionally "white and pink" and, in the more suggestive tradition of the eroticists of the early French seventeenth century, the Spanish ballerina painted by Manet in 1863 is said by Baudelaire to shine with "the charm of a pink and black jewel." Half of the *Fleurs du Mal* is tainted by prosaism, or strained in its imagery, or marred by a failure to achieve the purity and unity of tone for which Mallarmé has given us a taste not easily satisfied elsewhere.

But the other half remains unique in its depth and force: and some thirty or forty poems on the theme of love or of woman exemplify the originality of Baudelaire, all the more striking for having had to triumph over his lack of facility and over a certain poverty of imagination. Much has been made by some admirers of Baudelaire of his frequent and exalted hymns to imagination as "the queen of faculties," in formulas often borrowed from Delacroix. The word, as Margaret Gilman remarked, had, in contrast, remained almost absent from the many prefaces and aesthetic pronouncements of the French romantics, while, in Wordsworth, Coleridge, and Shelley it had been central in the speculations of their English predecessors. Baudelaire's praise of imagination is, nevertheless, deceptive. He coveted the gift which was possessed to a superlative degree by Delacroix, Balzac, and Hugo. He dreamed of composing novels and plays, for which the synthetic power of the mind imagining plot and characters is a prerequisite. But he wisely realized that his own gifts lay elsewhere. From his very deficiencies he knew how to draw strength. Memory, enriched with regret and nostalgia, and exasperated by the remorse which torments those who are aware of having whittled their lives away, took the place of imagination in his creative process. "Art is a mnemotechnics of the beautiful," he wrote in his 1846 *Salon,* and, in the celebrated essay on "The Painter of Modern Life," "the thought of the past is a thought which makes one mad."

His vocation was not to conjure up women as other love poets have done, endowing a Beatrice or a Laura with all the mysterious adornments imagined by their heart's desire. Nor was it to chant rapturous hymns to "L'amor che muove il sole e l'altre stelle" or to the ethereal love invoked in Shelley's *Epipsychidion.* Paul Valéry, with the acute discernment which is often provided by lack of sympathy, was clear-sighted when he made much of the sentence penned by Baudelaire in the first of his projected prefaces to *Les Fleurs du Mal:* "Illustrious poets had a long time ago apportioned among themselves the most flowery provinces of the poetical domain. It appeared attractive to me, and all the more so as the task was more arduous, to extract the *beauty* which lies in *Evil.*"

In his love poetry, Baudelaire delved more resolutely than any of his predecessors in verse into sensuality, the fascination and at the same time the horror of the flesh, the hatred of one's partner and accomplice and the need of inflicting pain, into self-hatred also and the delight of chastising oneself. He endowed that poetry with a new dimension through piercing many sentimental delusions, tearing veils of vapid platitudes, and thereby enabling it to suggest some of the infernal depths which the late eighteenth century (Laclos, Rétif, Sade) had opened up to prose fiction. But he was too great a psychologist to ignore the other facet of man's duality: his inveterate need for idealization, his metamorphosis of the woman desired and dreamed about, through the cerebral alchemy with which moderns delight in complicating lust or sentiment. If love must be, as Baudelaire often implies, suffering and "the certitude of doing *evil*," the analytical poet will endeavor to elicit the significance of such suffering, even to hail it as a divine blessing, "comme un divin remède à nos impuretés" ("Bénédiction"). He will gaze at the gulf separating the flesh from the spirit, but will also attempt to bridge that gulf through mystical correspondences. The most spiritual definition of the poet's role as a *"homo duplex"* is that which Baudelaire himself proposes in his *Salon* of the year 1859, when he wishes for him to declare: "I want to illumine things with my spirit and to project that reflection upon other spirits."

Likewise, and putting to advantage what he lucidly observed as his limitations, Baudelaire did not attempt to dazzle his readers with verbal pyrotechnics or with those cascades of jewels which were lavished by some Elizabethan poets, or by Hugo, or later by Rimbaud, and even by Saint John Perse in our time. The majority of his poems stay close to prose; they at times betray an inability to transmit the mysterious electrical current of "pure poetry" to a degree matched by no other major poet in French. The most inimical of Baudelaire's contemporaries did not err altogether when they mentioned his occasional resemblance to Boileau.[1] His affinity with the class-

---

[1] Baudelaire borrowed from E. A. Poe a dogmatic condemnation of "the didactic heresy" in poetry. Yet some of his most overvalued poems, such as "Le Voyage," are full of didactic messages: "Amer savoir, celui qu'on tire du voyage!" or "Etonnants voyageurs, quelles nobles histoires, / Nous lisons dans vos yeux profonds comme les mers!" Few lines of poetry are as atrociously infelicitous as the question put to "the offended moon," in "La Lune offensée," posthumously published: "Vois-tu les amoureux, sur leurs

ical poets of the seventeenth century is striking in his preference for abstract adjectives, almost totally devoid of color and of concrete picturesqueness, and in his resort to comparisons, introduced very traditionally through "comme," "ainsi que," "ressemble," "imite," "est l'emblème de." In contrast to such a pedestrian avoidance of evocativeness, in his most successful poems of love or of address to the woman desired and clad with the strangeness of his exotic dreams, Baudelaire unfolds majestic images, strange and yet imposed at once upon our disbelief and stifling it as inevitable. Proust, who admired them, was haunted by them and produced similar, though more diffuse, effects in his prose. "La Chevelure," for example, ascends, after several undulating movements, to the splendor of the final question:

> N'es-tu pas l'oasis où je rêve, et la gourde
> Où je hume à longs traits le vin du souvenir?

> Are you not the oasis where I dream, and the gourd
> From which, in long draughts, I sniff the wine of
> remembrance?

The brief poem which follows it in *Les Fleurs du Mal* opens, no less sumptuously, on a comparison which, while not new, is transformed into an evocative image blending the black woman, night, death into a mysterious penumbra:

> Je t'adore à l'égal de la voûte nocturne,
> O vase de tristesse, ô grande taciturne . . .

> I worship you as ardently as the nocturnal vault,
> O urn of sorrow, o great taciturn one . . .

---

grabats prospères. / De leur bouche en dormant montrer le frais émail." ("Do you see the lovers, prosperous on their dismal couches, / show while asleep the cool enamel in their mouths.")

A sonnet whose title, borrowed from Juvenal's imprecation against the most lustful woman of imperial Rome, "Sed non satiata" (fatigued by men, but not satiated, Messalina), appears at first to curse the insatiable mistress as a malevolent witch: it ends with an imploration for the woman to cease ordering that her lover be sapped of his whole substance for her. But the second quatrain spiritualizes that war in which hatred would soon engulf pleasure itself. The image of the dreary and parched desert in which the woman's eyes quench the lover's thirsty desire, like a delicious and perilous philter, is impregnated with a strange, purified sensuousness:

> Quand vers toi mes désirs partent en caravane,
> Tes yeux sont la citerne où boivent mes ennuis.

> When toward you my desires, caravan like, set out,
> Your eyes are the cistern from which my languorous
> griefs drink.

The life of Baudelaire has been explored in every one of its recesses. His literary sources have been more than generously tapped; there is barely a line of his poetry for which a more or less, usually less, precise similarity has not been detected in an earlier writer. E. A. Poe, J. de Maistre, Swedenborg, even Schelling and Hegel have been mentioned as having molded his thought. Most scholars know too much and are reluctant to accept the obvious: that in the arts, in poetry as in science, there is far less borrowing than they think, and far more of a simultaneous appearance of ideas, themes, images, phrases, all through a process of polygenesis. If Baudelaire, or any other original author, borrowed or found hidden in the recesses of his mind and half consciously re-emerging some phrases once read elsewhere, only the subterranean work through which he transmuted such dross into gold need detain us. The reader of English poets may feel tempted to compare the sudden enchantment with which some of Baudelaire's love sonnets open with Shakespearean first lines:

Shall I compare thee to a summer's day . . .

or

When to the sessions of sweet silent thought . . .

At other times, he is struck by analogies with lines in Donne or in Blake. Analogies indeed they are, and not sources. And a prudent exploration of affinities between creators who, time and space being disregarded, belong to the same family of spirits may prove more enlightening to a psychological critic than the delving into sources.

Lived sources are obviously far more revealing than bookish ones where love is concerned. Everything has been said about the several women whom Baudelaire loved: the black Venus, Mme Sabatier, the girl with the golden hair. Much less is known about the three or four others to whom he alludes in his verse. We need not deplore it overmuch. Goethe's brutal epigram is true also for natures other than Goethe's egotistic one, slowly gaining sensual gratification and mental wisdom through his "Lehrjahre": "Women are silver bowls on which men lay golden apples." The sonnet which closed the original edition of the *Fleurs du Mal,* "La Mort des Artistes," contains one of the few revelations which the poet allowed himself on his conception of the artist's role. Artists have to multiply experiments and trials, must shoot many arrows in vain, before hitting a goal "of mystical nature" and perhaps altogether illusory. The attachment which, notwithstanding violent quarrels, Baudelaire felt for nearly twenty years for Jeanne Duval, his mulatto mistress—"all my pleasures and all my duties" as he termed her—may be difficult for us to understand. It did not, however, surprise his friends overmuch; and little good is achieved by gratuitous speculations on its physical basis or on Baudelaire's sexual deficiencies.

It need only be recalled that, unlike Goethe or Hugo, Baudelaire never was, in love, an indefatigable conqueror. He might rather be ranked among those à propos of whom an English poet, James Thomson, equally fascinated by the power of blackness and by artificial paradises, wrote: "Lips only sing when they cannot kiss." Like Gide, probably also like Stendhal and the not overly virile character of *She Stoops to Conquer,* Baudelaire disassociated adoration and pleasure. He saw something debasing (of the woman partner and of the lover) in carnal violence, probably, like Proust, a profanation of the mother image. The act of love had to appear like a Goyaesque fight of two sorcerers or like a duel of two warriors. "O fureur des cœurs mûrs par l'amour ulcérés!" ("O fury of mature hearts exacerbated by love!"), he exclaims in the sonnet "Duellum." Through fear of love and of woman's physical demands, probably also through a curiosity which we coyly call morbid, the poet may well have been inclined to be a voyeur rather than a doer. He was fascinated enough by Lesbian loves and "le cantique muet que chante le plaisir" ("the mute canticle sung by pleasure") of women embracing to have thought of choosing "Les Lesbiennes" as the title to the whole volume. Probably, like many so-called Latin males, and as a reader of Stendhal, he was haunted by the fear of momentary sexual impotence and was thus inclined to set up the woman on a pedestal, adorned with jewels in her nudity, and to leave her there. Such worship at a safe distance, which other egotists concerned with nurturing their inspiration and polishing their style (Flaubert, Rilke) have preferred, hailing love's best as the epistolary exchange of two solitudes, would have kept the metallic goddess "De troubler le repos où mon âme était mise" ("from disturbing the rest in which my soul was laid"). Much else may be read into Baudelaire's way of loving: a Catholic sense of love as sin and of woman as the forbidden one; at the same time, obsessive reveries about the other sex. Baudelaire's father, it has recently been proved beyond doubt, had been a priest before the Revolution and the son's friends often compared his dress and his behavior to those of a seminarist. Sartre, on the other hand, has stressed Baudelaire's obstinate refusal to project himself, in Existentialist fashion, and to forget about his past and his class and affirm his own values. Strangely enough, for Sartre's attitude to love is that of a Jansenist who renders the flesh ugly and sensual union horrifying. This twentieth-century philosopher, who extolled Genet, upbraided Baudelaire for not having dared rise above the contingencies of his class and of his sexual inhibitions. Both of them were among those many Frenchmen who, when their widowed mother marries again, decide they must feel as Hamlet did. But the picture of love, alternately tender, devoted, idealizing, or brutal and associated with death which Baudelaire drew in his verse, is infinitely richer and psychologically truer, as well as deeper, than any which can emerge from the dozen plays and novels by anti-Baudelairian Sartre. "Le Balcon," "Ciel brouillé," "Chant d'Automne," "Les Bijoux," "Le Jet d'eau" and twenty other poems of supreme beauty amply justify Baudelaire for having deliberately refused to assume his freedom and ruined his actual life, in order to leave to posterity that legacy, "Vaisseau favorisé par un grand aquilon" ("vessel favored by a great northern wind").

Baudelaire's love poetry, unlike that of others, has successfully shunned one of the perils of that theme in literature, and perhaps of love itself as expressed in letters, terms of endearment, compliments, scenes and gestures in real life; monotony. It embraces the domains of the sensual, the sentimental, and the cerebral.

Sensuality was not absent from Catullus and from Ovid. It was refined and half concealed in Petrarch, frank, occasionally brutal in the French poets of the Renaissance, more overt still in the neo-Latin poetry of Jean Second or in Marlowe's *Hero and Leander.* In a more subtle form, and at times sensuous rather than sensual (the French language, in all that pertains to sex and love, is less precise and poorer than the English, and both adjectives are rendered by the one "sensuel"), Milton and Marlowe have admitted sensuality into their poetry; Coleridge applied the three adjectives, "simple, sensuous and passionate" to the author of *Paradise Lost,* and the first one, "simple," is doubtless the only one which is hardly fitting. With the intrusion of eroticism into the literature of the second half of the eighteenth century (into fiction far more than into poetry), a cerebral and voluptuous view of sensuality has become a characteristic of modernity. If poetry were not to lag behind the fiction of Laclos and Sade (even behind the reminiscences of Rousseau and of Casanova), it had to become analytical, complex, often suggestive. As a rule, Baudelaire eschewed the coarser sensuality of the poets of the seventeenth century, such as Théophile, whom his friends revived and praised; scorn of the woman as Martial in Latin and the libertine poets of 1610–1640 had crudely professed may have entertained Flaubert and friend Louis Bouilhet, among Baudelaire's contemporaries, but it ill fitted the gravity of the singer of evil as a proof of original sin tainting man's corrupt nature. Even the final wrathful stanzas of "A celle qui est trop gaie" evince respect for the woman whose healthy cheerfulness unnerved her poet-lover.

The sensuality present in the volume of poems (it is not found in the poems in prose or in any of Baudelaire's stories or essays on opium and hashish) is often that which appealed to the Petrarchists once, and to the Surrealists more recently. Like them, Baudelaire sketches enumerations of the physical charms of the woman: unlike them, he dwells seldom on the cheeks and the teeth and even the neck which, in some Italian paintings, could be made so poetically languid. The "gorge," as the French used to designate the broad and bulging front in women which least deserves to be compared to a narrow pass, occasionally serves as a pretext for a more precise evocation of a beauty à la Rubens. "Le Beau Navire," in which the woman harmoniously walking is likened to a majestic ship unfurling its sails, is the most curiously sustained catalogue of the beauties of the ample woman addressed. It must have been written for Marie Daubrun who, presumably, felt flattered to see her arms pictured as powerful serpents, capable of stifling "precocious Hercules." Her shoulders also are fat ("grasses" rhymes conveniently in French with "grâces"). But the breastplates of her bosom are especially conspicuous, in lines which are not, in my opinion, too successful as poetry but curiously baroque in their far-fetched imagery:

> Ta gorge triomphante est une belle armoire
> Dont les panneaux bombés et clairs
> Comme les boucliers accrochent des éclairs;
>
> Boucliers provoquants, armés de pointes roses!

> Your triumphant bust is a splendid wardrobe
> Whose bulging and clear panels
> Like shields catch lightning;
> Provoking shields, armed with rosy points!

The only other piece in which the poet indulged a similar catalogue of a woman's physical charms is clearly a buffoonery and was published under that general category in the posthumous edition of *Les Fleurs du Mal,* "Le Monstre." Its tone is humorous and deliberately vulgar and it reveals Baudelaire as a master of sarcasm. Generally, however, a thin or lean woman appears to have better corresponded to his ideal of feminine beauty. He would have relished Modigliani's women and, had he known his works better, those of Lucas Cranach. "La maigreur," he wrote, and the French substantive conveys more than thinness or leanness, "is more bare, more indecent than fatness." A poet whom he knew, August Lacaussade, had advanced, perhaps with involuntary humor, that "on est plus près du cœur quand la poitrine est plate" ("One is closer to the heart when the breast is flat").

In the same poem, "Le Beau Navire," Baudelaire alluded to the swinging rhythm of the woman's gait, conveyed somewhat in an unusual and skillfully balanced stanza, and to the legs of the woman, expert at tormenting or teasing the desires of the male. Repeatedly, he is fascinated by the rhythm of a woman's walk, enhanced by the gowns then worn by Parisian ladies, with flounces and festoons, "sweeping the air" or gracefully held and swung by the woman's hand.[2] Baudelaire, however, never stresses the geometry of feminine legs as a promise of higher secrets to tantalize the male observer. Proust remarked in his article on Baudelaire that the poet often accused of morbidity chastely stops at the knees of the woman; like the suppliant before an Egyptian statue of a goddess, or even more like a child yearning for motherly solace, he asks

---

[2] One of the most dramatic sonnets of *Les Fleurs du Mal,* addressed to "une passante," an anonymous woman seen for a minute only crossing a Paris street, pictures her "d'une main fastueuse, soulevant, balançant le feston et l'ourlet" ("with a fastuous hand, lifting, swinging hems and festoons").

to lay his weary forehead on the woman's lap: "Ah! Laissez-moi, le fronte posé sur vos genoux" ("Chant d'automne") or, at the end of "Le Voyage," "Dit celle dont jadis nous baisions les genoux" ("Ah! let me, my brow laid on your lap . . . says she whose knees we once kissed").

The woman's hair set Baudelaire's fancy roaming more than any other part or accessory of the female body. Every culture has its peculiar love ritual and stresses, in its poetry, one or another aspect of the person courted and lauded. English love poetry appears to have shied away from the uppermost part of a woman standing, the hair. Baudelaire's fascination with the hair, rapturously conveyed in "La Cheve-lure" and in the prose poem in which he hails a whole hemi-sphere in the waving hair of his mistress, proved contagious. The theme will, after him, haunt Mallarmé, Maeterlinck in a famous scene of *Pelléas et Mélisande,* Proust and even Claudel's Mesa when he alludes to Ysé's "chevelure" or watches her combing it when he last visits her, before being himself visited by God and by death. The hair was, to the singer of Jeanne Duval, a receptacle of perfumes which con-jured up exotic lands. It was, as for the Greek sculptors of old and several modern French painters, the most changeable and, blown by the wind like "the bright hair uplifted from the head of some fierce Maenad," in the Shelleyan phrase, the most alive element of a woman's personality. For those poets who appreciate nature best when it is humanized, the woman's hair stands for the most vegetal part of the human being, the one which they can compare to long silky grasses as Proust does and which serves as an intercessor between nature and the male, that animal with short hair and long ideas as he insisted on appearing in the nineteenth century. For Baude-laire, even the fragrance of the hair is hardly a pretext for sensuous reveries; he cherishes Jeanne Duval's dark tresses be-

cause they are replete with memories which he wants to trea-
sure and to revive, and because of the dreams of travels, presumably solitary, which the hair provokes:

> Tu contiens, mer d'ébène, un éblouissant rêve
> De voiles, de rameurs, de flammes et de mâts.

> You contain, sea of ebony, a scintillating dream
> Of sails and rowers, of pennants and of masts.

Even more than the hair, the eyes of the woman, half veiled
with languor or dimmed with tears, seldom brightly alive or
saucily provoking, more often dreamy and indolent, are the
theme of Baudelaire's most poetical hymns. The eyes of Mme
Sabatier or those of Marie Daubrun (he easily transferred to
one the poems written for, or on, the other), rather than the
colder gaze of his mulatto mistress, have inspired those lines.
Coldness there is, in those eyes of a Gorgon-like woman,
inexpressive, petrifying, "charming minerals": if the hair
appealed to the poet's "vegetable love," the metallic eyes, re-
calling the statuesque Beauty in the sonnet "La Beauté,"
affirmed the woman's closeness to inanimate stone. In "Le
Serpent qui danse," where the woman is likened both to a
snake and to a ship, he celebrates her eyes in unusual fashion:

> Tes yeux, où rien ne se révèle
>   De doux ni d'amer,
> Sont deux bijoux froids où se mêle
>   L'or avec le fer.

> Your eyes, where nothing sweet or bitter is revealed,
>   are two cold jewels in which gold and iron are
>   mixed.

In "Le Poison," the same green eyes, lakes in which his soul
trembles to see itself reflected in reverse, emit a venom.

Elsewhere the color of the eyes is less clearly determined. It reflects the changing moods of the mysterious person and perhaps the paleness of the sky on days when clouds tarnish the sun's brightness. One of the most tender invocations to the loved one in the whole volume occurs at the opening of "Ciel brouillé":

> On dirait ton regard, d'une vapeur couvert;
> Ton œil mystérieux (est-il bleu, gris ou vert?)
> Alternativement tendre, rêveur, cruel,
> Réfléchit l'indolence et la pâleur du ciel.

> One would say your gaze is veiled in a mist; Your mysterious eye (is it blue, grey or green), alternately tender, dreamy, cruel, reflects the indolence and the paleness of the sky.

Less original is the idealized celebration of the eyes as the windows of the soul or as the luminous and living torches guiding the worshipping lover, as in the rapturous sonnet "Le Flambeau vivant," in the least natural manner of Edgar Allan Poe or of the rapturous and disembodied canzone of the *Vita Nuova*. Any sensuality is excluded from those Baudelairian raptures inspired by Mme Sabatier, or any suggestion of desire. Once at least, in the most expertly musical of all his poems, "Le Jet d'eau," the poet, purifying but retaining the sensual element, alluded to the eyes of the woman after love has fulfilled her: they are half closed and dazed, and rocked by the sound of the fountain, in the courtyard, which, ascending in the air and descending rhythmically, prolongs the ecstasy which the two lovers experienced.

> Tes beaux yeux sont las, pauvre amante!
> Reste longtemps sans les rouvrir,
> Dans cette pose nonchalante

Où t'a surprise le plaisir.
Dans la cour le jet d'eau qui jase
Et ne se tait ni nuit ni jour
Entretient doucement l'extase
Où ce soir m'a plongé l'amour ...

> Your lovely eyes are weary, poor lover! Stay a long
> while without opening them again, in that non-
> chalant pose in which pleasure by surprise seized
> you. In the courtyard the babbling fountain, which
> night and day runs on, softly prolongs the ecstasy
> into which tonight love plunged me.

Most often however, more probably than in any other great
poet's work, unfulfilled love, with its exasperation of desire,
is the subject of Baudelaire's poems, and the part played by
the senses is extenuated in them. Goethe, in his *Xenien,*
extolled the "delicious poison of unfulfilled love," "das Gift
der unbefriedigten Liebe," which burns and cools, corrodes
the marrow of the bone and renews it. But the marked restraint showed by Baudelaire in avoiding any frank delineation
of love fully accomplished is not the only means through
which he controls sensuality in his poetry. Jean Prévost,
in his posthumous book, the best in French on Baudelaire,
has shrewdly analyzed some of the devices he used to under-
play the role of desire in love and to deprive the war of the
two sexes of any suggestion of brutality. His few poems on a
nude body, especially "Les Bijoux" which frightened the courts
of justice in 1857, are characteristically cold, even colder than
Manet's "Olympia" which likewise revolted the timorous
onlookers of the French Second Empire. The reclining
woman wearing her jewels as a foil for her nudity becomes a

work of art, but arouses neither desire nor fear of those failures which the poet dreaded.

Another feature of the Baudelairian feminine ideal is sadness. The poet could conceive beauty only as "ardent and melancholy." Cheerfulness irritated him, presumably as slightly vulgar and detracting from the Jansenist gravity with which love should be imprinted. The variegated colors of the woman's dresses and her insolent health, in "A Celle qui est trop gaie," drive her admirer to anger and wickedness. He prefers his female companion to be clad with a mantle of sadness and ennobled by it.

He also prefers her not to be too talkative. There are no dialogues in Baudelaire's love poems, not even in "Confession" where he records a few complaints whispered by the woman on the role which she must constantly put on (the complaints are trite, it must be admitted) or in the opening lines of "Semper eadem" in which, again, the woman wonders why she is invaded by gloom. He answers her by a invitation to silence. "Et, bien que votre voix soit douce, taisez-vous!" She is but a child and should know that men prefer to intoxicate themselves with a lie, which is only possible if their female partner keeps her lips sealed. "Be lovely and be sad," he bids the woman; "Sois belle! et sois triste! Les pleurs/Ajoutent un charme au visage,/Comme le fleuve au paysage" ("Tears add a charm to the face, as the river does to the landscape"). That very original poem in octosyllabic lines is entitled "Madrigal triste"; it expresses insistently the poet's requirement of tears "as warm as blood" and of silence in the beloved. John Donne likewise, but more brutally, had begun one of his love poems, "The Canonization," with the line:

For God's sake, hold your tongue, and let me love.

Being able to dream about love rather than to act it is Baudelaire's preference.[3]

Indeed, a pathetic fear runs through that strange love poetry where sensuality is repeatedly subdued and the impetuosity of desire offset or annihilated: it is the fear of passion and of anything which might disrupt the regular order of life and the poet's normalcy. Here again, the contrast between Baudelaire and his successors is striking. He wrote magnificently on hashish and opium, but to condemn those artificial paradises and the disorder which they stir, in severely moralistic tones. After him, Rimbaud, then the Surrealists, did not hesitate to proclaim as "sacred the disorder of their minds." Rather than possession, passion, and domination, mutual understanding is what Baudelaire prizes in his relations with women. Too much may be made, and has been made, of his close dependency upon his mother. The words "a complex" need not be pronounced, and contribute little in the way of an explanation. But, again like Proust, and with more slyness (for he had to implore his mother for money incessantly), Baudelaire cajoled and deceived his mother, and looked for maternal tenderness and protection in the women whom he addressed in verse.

Et pourtant aimez-moi, tendre cœur! Soyez mère . . .

And yet love me, tender heart! Be a mother . . .

he begs her in "Chant d'automne." In several poems, he invokes, in the same breath, the mistress as a sister, yearning for fraternal affection and gentle understanding more than for passionate love, as in "Chant d'automne":

---

[3] "Sois charmante et tais-toi" ("Be charming and keep silent"), he repeats in "Sonnet d'automne" and in the eighth line of the same sonnet he makes the curious avowal: "Je hais la passion . . ." ("I hate passion . . .").

Amante ou sœur, soyez la douceur éphemère
D'un glorieux automne ou d'un soleil couchant

Lover or sister, be the ephemeral sweetness
Of a glorious autumn or of a setting sun

Sensuality is ever present in that poetry of love, but also ever held in check, feared or sublimated. The two other features which make up the originality of Baudelaire are his stress on the cerebral element in modern man which analyzes and complicates desire, and the resort to imagination which raises obstacles and heightens love, otherwise a vulgar and almost animal affair in the eyes of a poet.

One of the earliest critics who wrote on Baudelaire with some penetration and hailed him as the inspirer of the young was Paul Bourget. The essay which he published almost twenty years after the poet's death in a magazine, then in his *Essais de Psychologie contemporaine,* had a section on "the spirit of analysis in love" which *Les Fleurs du Mal* had introduced into poetry. The romantics had not, in France, and still less in England and Germany (nor had Leopardi), ignored the power of the inquisitive and self-tormenting intellect to multiply and intensify joy or pain. In general, however, they had been drawn to the world without rather than to the world within. Ronsard, Sidney, and Donne had likewise been more than once lucid observers of their own emotions and sentiments. Donne in particular had treated them with irony and even his own death as "love's martyr" is contemplated without any self-pity. But self-knowledge in the very midst of passionate feelings came to be a requirement of love poetry around the middle of the nineteenth century, if that poetry was to satisfy, with a rich psychological content, the readers of Rousseau, Laclos, Stendhal, Balzac. With a lag of three or four decades or more, the poetry of Matthew Arnold, Browning, Meredith, that of Baudelaire, around 1850–1860, attempted to catch up with the psychological refinements which fiction had appropriated; so did the theatre, but with less success and too often by replacing psychological analysis, which tends to be static, with moral conflicts and with social preaching (Augier, Dumas fils, Ibsen, G. B. Shaw). A literary history which, disregarding actual influences and chronological or vertical sequence, were to explore simultaneous and parallel moods in countries impervious to each other might throw greater light on the emergence of trends in thought or in sensibility. Baudelaire was composing his verse in the early eighteen fifties and published them in a volume in 1857. In England, around the same time, there had appeared *Sonnets from the Portuguese* (1850), Tennyson's *Maud* (1853), Browning's *Men and Women* and the second series of Arnold's *Poems* in 1855, James Thomson's first prose rhapsody on death, *Our Ladies of Death,* in 1861, and Meredith's *Modern Love* in 1862. Swinburne, the only English poet who knew and praised Baudelaire, was then preparing his explosive *Poems and Ballads,* which caused a scandal in Victorian England in 1866. Through those English poems, even in Mrs. Browning's sonnets, love was dissected even more than it was celebrated. Searching intellects probed into its sensual excesses (Swinburne), its closeness to insanity (Tennyson), its brotherhood with death (Wagner's *Tristan* was completed in 1859). Never had relentless self-knowledge in poetry been pursued as it was then by Browning and by Baudelaire, in all other respects poles apart, on the two sides of the Channel. It is to be regretted that the ban on Baudelaire as morbid and decadent, well nigh universal then in France, prevented Browning's French friend, Milsand, from initiating him to *Les Fleurs du Mal.*

Baudelaire might have read, in one of the most curious novels of Balzac, *Béatrix,* of the enormous role of will power in the crystallizing process which precedes and secretes love. More probably, he had perceived or experienced that voluntary delusion early in his thoughtful life. That will to believe and to be deluded was stronger in him than the will for concentration, for which he always prayed in vain. As early as the age of twenty-six, in *La Fanfarlo,* he attributed to his double, Samuel Cramer, cynical declarations on love which drew tears from the lady whom the young dandy was trying to interest: "The most saddening thing is that any love always makes a poor ending, all the poorer as it had, at its beginning, been more divine and wingèd." The last stanza of the poem, appositely entitled "L'Amour du mensonge," offers a pathetic revelation:

Mais ne suffit-il pas que tu sois l'apparence,
Pour réjouir un cœur qui fuit la vérité?

But is it not enough that you should be the mere
    appearance,
To give joy to a heart which will not hear the truth?

Proustian heroes act in perfect Baudelairian fashion, when they deliberately launch into the love affair which is most sure to be a source of torture, because such anguish is better than solitude and than the bliss of ignorance; it opens the road to self-knowledge.

Baudelairian love, fearful of unleashing desire, anxious to disarm it, deprives the senses so as to enrich the intellectual element in love. Such a process of intellectualizing results in a new and more insidious superexcitation. Hence that lack of power to love, which Benjamin Constant had been the first to probe in *Adolphe:* the inner force which might have been projected on to the partner and perhaps have spent itself in carnal fulfillment is thrown back upon the lover himself and devours his thoughts and his nightmares. Hence also the enhancing of eroticism, of which one facet is the lover's eagerness to observe and thus to share his partner's experience in the love act, while analyzing his own. In almost religious language and in austere and abstract terms, Baudelaire depicted the two Lesbian women, in the amplest and most majestic piece in the volume ("Femmes damnées"), performing a gloomy ritual. A will to be worshipped as the giver of pleasure impels Delphine, the older and stronger of that feminine couple, as she watches her accomplice and victim:

> Elle cherchait dans l'œil de sa pâle victime
> Le cantique muet que chante le plaisir
> Et cette gratitude infinie et sublime
> Qui sort de la paupière ainsi qu'un long soupir.

> She looked, in the eye of her pallid victim,
> For the mute canticle which pleasure sings,
> And that infinite and sublime gratitude
> Which comes out of the eyelid like a long sigh.

That cerebral introspection is not that of a detached observer who might relish watching the workings of his brain and the mechanism of his self-delusion. It never shakes itself free from moral judgment and from the conviction that love is evil and that celebrating its rites, or merely being tempted to yield to it, is fundamentally becoming a prey to Satan's machinations. T. S. Eliot in England and some ardent French Catholics have depicted Baudelaire as "a Christian born out of his due time," or even as a saint. His sensibility certainly was permeated by that conception of Christianity which brandishes woman as a snare of the Devil and love as a form of metaphysical evil. The most terrifying lines in the *Fleurs du Mal* are not the conventional ones in which the woman is vituperated against as a vampire, but the picture of consciousness delving into its own recesses, becoming also the moral conscience which judges and condemns, facing evil ironically cursed and cherished:

> Tête à tête sombre et limpide,
> Qu'un cœur devenu son miroir!
> Puits de vérité clair et noir
> Où tremble une étoile livide,
>
> Un phare ironique, infernal,
> Flambeau de grâces sataniques,
> Soulagement et gloire uniques,
> —La conscience dans le Mal!
>
> Sombre and limpid confrontation,
> A heart which is its own mirror!
> Clear and black well of truth
> In which a livid star trembles,
>
> Ironical and infernal beacon,
> Torch of Satan's graces,
> Unique solace and glory,
> —Consciousness in Evil itself!

The three forms assumed by evil thus pictured as an active force are aggressiveness in love unleashed by either of the two partners, self-destruction wrought by the male in his masochist wrath, and the attraction of death as the one logical goal and end of love.

The poems alluding to the woman's blood-sucking fury

and to her perversely capricious onslaughts on the male's physical energy and on his quietude belong to a tradition of vampirism, of which the late and minor French romantics were the inheritors. They do not constitute the deeper part of Baudelaire's love poems. Cursing the female enemy dispenses the poet from lending to her any character. But two of the most masterly pieces in *Les Fleurs du Mal* show the man wreaking his revenge upon the insatiable woman. One, "A Celle qui est trop gaie," has already been alluded to: its octosyllabic lines grouped in stanzas of four create an impression of glee even where the poet's thirst for chastisement of the overly gay woman ascends to the tragic, animal-like inflicting of a wound. The other one, "Une Martyre," was singled out by Paul Bourget, as early as 1883, as "the most powerful in the volume." Nothing in Poe or in Swinburne, or in Elizabethan dramatists like Ford and Webster, could match the lurid and ironical grandeur of the scene. The martyr is not a martyr to faith, not even to love: she lies, amid a voluptuous and refined setting, beheaded: the crime has just taken place and the pillow is soaked with her blood. The headless body still wears part of the feminine clothing which her aggressor must have torn. After drawing a picture which Goya or Delacroix would not have disowned, Baudelaire, as he often does, meditates on the sight. Generalizing remarks and rhetorical questions follow: the poet would like to hear her answer to soothe his morbid curiosity. Did her lover and murderer satisfy his too immense lust on her "inert and submissive flesh?" The finale proposes a moral lesson, very much as Proust's scenes of sadism do or his strange essay on the son who, out of love, butchered his mother: her murderer has sealed the rites of marriage through his deed and, unto the last, he will now remain faithful to his victim. In no other Flower of Evil have dramatic force and pictorial vividness been so harmoniously blended; in none has "the tempestuous loveliness of terror," of which Shelley speaks apropos of the Medusa attributed to Leonardo da Vinci, been so terrifying.

Baudelaire never heard of Sader Masoch, his contemporary who published in French magazines a few years after the poet's death. But self-destruction was practiced long before it received the name of that strange Austro-Hungarian. The sonnet "La Destruction," the starkest of the masochistic poems, with a Demon maddening and humiliating the victim, is hardly a love poem, even if it may be read as referring to onanism. "L'Heautontimoroumenos," entitled after a play by Menander done over in Latin by Terence, is less graphically concrete. The punishment which the executioner-poet wants to inflict on his mistress is mental rather than physical; it is paralleled by the even more furious punishment which, as a vampire of himself, he wreaks upon himself. He suffers in her body as well as in his own.

> Je suis la plaie et le couteau!
> Je suis le soufflet et la joue!
>
> I am the wound and the knife!
> I am the slap and the cheek!

The awareness of the obstacles of aggression and self-destruction which Baudelairian love requires in order to avoid insipidity dramatizes the sensual reveries of the poet; his cerebral eroticism adds spice to the monotony of a love which would be free from self-hatred and from sadism. Death, however, is the supreme fulfillment. Ever since Petrarch, the triumph of death over all human emotions has been sung by poets. Leopardi, in whom Baudelaire should have hailed a brotherly poet (Musset praised that "sombre lover of death" and Lacaussade quoted him often), has a Canto on "Amore e Morte."

In *Les Fleurs du Mal,* the horror of the body's corruption is linked with the blasting of the delusions of love, in cruel poems like "La Béatrice" and "Un Voyage à Cythère." The hideousness depicted there is a little conventional, the appeal to Death as the captain of the outward bound ship, once all other peregrinations have been dismissed as fruitless, in "Le Voyage" (in my opinion one of the most artificially composed and least evocative pieces in the whole volume) sounds rhetorical. The most poetical and rare moment in which Baudelaire marries love and death in a dreamy, almost pre-Raphaelite setting, again producing a delicate pictorial effect with the angel of some funereal annunciation visiting the two dead lovers, is "La Mort des Amants." Seldom has the decasyllabic verse, one of the most difficult to wield effectively in French, been treated with such unobtrusive mastery. The unity of tone is preserved throughout the fourteen lines, an uncommon feat in Baudelaire who usually aimed at discordant changes of style or who found it difficult to maintain a smooth purity of imagery throughout fourteen lines. The first tercet alone need be quoted here, perhaps the one Baudelairian moment where (in death, however) pleasure and love are both mutually experienced and not exclusive of one another:

> Un soir fait de rose et de bleu mystique,
> Nous échangerons un éclair unique,
> Comme un long sanglot, tout chargé d'adieux . . .

> On an evening made of rose and mystical blue,
> We shall exchange a unique flashing glimpse,
> Like a long sob overladen with adieux . . .

Too much has been made, and not only by the critics who, for several decades after his death, viewed him as decadent, of the nostalgia of the mud in Baudelaire's poetry. The movement toward the lower and murky depths in us, with its delving into abysses of sensuality and of fear, is indeed one of the original features of his delineation of love, which makes other poets appear timorous in comparison and poor in symbolic secrets. But the Baudelairian correspondences rise boldly above such frightened contemplation of the flesh and of the demoniacal. The poet displayed equal courage when he dared, Icarus-like, soar into the empyrean and even, Ixion-like, embrace clouds of ethereal phantoms. From the modern city and its turbulence, from its mud and its dens of evil, he was proud of having extracted, like a chemist, the epic poetry and the purest gold. We may well mourn his never having completed the sketch for an epilogue to *Les Fleurs du Mal* which would have closed on the famous lines:

> Car j'ai de chaque chose extrait la quintessence;
> Tu m'as donné ta boue et j'en ai fait de l'or.

> For I have, from each object, extracted the quintessence;
> You gave to me your mud, I turned it into gold.

In his prose essays, from which the most original poetics of the French nineteenth century may be pieced together, Baudelaire had multiplied peremptory statements such as this one: "Any lyrical poet, in virtue of his nature, fatally works out a return toward a lost Eden. Everything, men, landscapes, palaces, in the lyrical world, becomes, so to speak, *apotheosized*" (on Théodore de Banville). Literally, the poet is a forger of gods and of goddesses. Through damnation, he gropes for salvation. Through the flesh, tortured, maligned, scorned, he reaches toward spirituality. "Dans la brute assoupie un ange se réveille" from "L'Aube spirituelle": "In the slumbering brute an angel awakens." Some critics have endeavored to sum up Baudelaire in that process of bipolarity, showing him, by dint of highly scientific terms and of counts of his verbal devices, oscillating from a negative to a positive pole. No mechanical interpretation of that sort can suit the man who condemned all systems as much too comfortable structures of half lies.

Simply, by the side of aggressivity which may lurk in sensual union, and of the cerebrality which revels in exacerbating it, there exists also in the Baudelairian man the sentiment which prolongs passion; there is generosity and the assumption of a duty on the part of the male lover. In that extraordinarily pure and tender elegy, "Le Balcon," addressed to the mulatto woman, he does not hesitate to invoke her, in the second line, as "ô toi, tous mes devoirs." No love poem in Musset, Hugo, Nerval, Verlaine, or Apollinaire is impregnated with that reasonable tenderness which Baudelaire invested with re-strained imagery, always eschewing the vulgarity which we tend to associate with sentimentality. The famous Platonic elevation at the end of "Une Charogne," the "Hymne" which invokes Mme Sabatier as "l'ange, l'idole immortelle" ("the angel, the immortal idol"), the plaintive stanzas probably composed for Marie Daubrun ("Chant d'automne") do not emit a harsh note as the poet's vituperations of scorn and hatred often did. Death itself has lost its sting and its hope of being victorious. Love is triumphant.

Its triumph is achieved through understanding the partner, submitting to her with humility, transfiguring her through imagination, and also through the alchemy of memory. With Baudelaire, then with Apollinaire, Proust, Alain Fournier, Mauriac, whose imagination is too weak or too firmly held in check by the writer, memory replaces imagination in the elaboration of the work of art. Those typically modern men cannot forget all that lies behind them, in their childhood and in their dreams of fond security in that "green paradise." Proust repeats that the only true paradises are the lost ones. Baudelaire could not be consoled for having been exiled from the bliss once dreamed of: he pictures the poet as essentially "a nature exiled in the world of imperfection, and wanting to conquer immediately, on this very earth, a revealed paradise" (*New Notes on E. A. Poe*). Like Proust again, and unlike either Bergson or Sartre for whom living is acting and molding the future, Baudelaire's inner gaze is fascinated by the past. The lover embracing the body of his mistress does not, in the poem "Un Fantôme," necessarily experience pleasure; he plucks the exquisite flower of memory. Like the perfume which intoxicates us through restoring and enshrining the past into the present,

> Ainsi l'amant sur un corps adoré
> Du souvenir cueille la fleur exquise.

Experience may be disappointing or, as for Proust, too brutally unpoetical, unprepared by imaginative anticipation, to be pleasurable. But, sublimated by the alchemy of memory and of regret, it will someday be a source of joy. Aeneas consoled himself likewise with the oft-quoted: "Forsan . . . olim meminisse juvabit," probably a rephrasing of a line from Euripides' *Andromeda.*

The limitations of Baudelairian love poetry have implicitly been marked in the preceding pages. The chief one is, but for rare exceptions like "Le Jet d'eau" (and even there a gentle melancholy creeps in), the reluctance or the inability to express joy. Claudel has indicted the poetry of the whole nineteenth century for its repudiation of joy: religious and mystical, purely human joy, even that sprightliness which Wordsworth knew in the contemplation of daffodils or Byron in rolling once again upon the ocean. The delight most often sung is that of solitariness: nature alone affords genuine solace to poets wounded by passion and by society. An anthology of the poetry of joy would indeed be a sad enterprise; most poets, and probably many men, cannot truly live up to the "carpe diem" and not appear selfish or shallow. "If joy is better than sorrow, joy is not great," declared arch-pessimist Robinson Jeffers, opening his finest short poem. Eighteenth-century poets had attempted to sing happy love and wine and to proffer invitations to Cytherea to ladies envious of shepherdesses. Goethe had succeeded best in his brief poem to Frau von Stein, in 1781:

> Euch bedaur'ich, unglückselige Sterne, . . .
> Denn ihr liebt nicht, kanntet nie die Liebe!

> I pity you, unhappy stars, . . .
> For you do not love, never have you known love!

But the more sensual joy sung during his Roman nights with a less majestic lady than Frau von Stein, in his *Römische Elegien,* is not untainted with coarseness. Baudelaire did not even try to sing hymns to joy. Perhaps he wisely understood that music alone can convey bliss.

The second gap in Baudelaire's otherwise varied gallery of love poems is the small attention he pays to the reactions, feelings, inner turmoils of the feminine partner in the liaison. It is easier either to idealize and to patronize the loved one as an angel or a weak creature in need of protection, or else to declaim against her wiles and her vampire's greed: to imagine her as an equal, talking back to the man, spurning his idealization and preferring to be known and loved for what she is may be a more arduous enterprise. No romantic poet in France tried to have the woman explain herself poetically, nor did Apollinaire, Eluard, or Char later. Only a dramatic monologue, of the kind that Robert Browning wrote, could incorporate enough psychological analysis and tension in lengthy love poems to make them the equals in self-awareness and in the understanding of the fairer, and silent sex, of modern novels. There is nowhere in Baudelaire the equivalent of "Any Wife to Any Husband" or of that other splendid Browning piece, "In a Year."

A third requirement of the moderns, accustomed to many novels in which the diverse phases of passion are minutely analyzed, is not fulfilled by Baudelaire's poetry, nor is it in most poetry where the perils to love are jealousy, the coquetry of the woman, her prudishness, her fickleness, or simply the male's weariness: that is, their need to explore the process of "désamour." Falling out of love is lengthier, more insidious, less naive than falling in love. Decrystallization is even more mysterious than the phenomenon to which Stendhal gave that now famous name of crystallization. Poets have, in Swinburnian fashion, traditionally lamented that love has an end and that

> Even the weariest river
> Winds somewhere safe to sea.

But how? Why? And, far more tragic than hatred or revenge is the total indifference which can replace ardent passion. Baudelaire, the most analytical and clear-sighted of French poets, steered clear of such questions, all the more regrettably in our eyes as he had wanted to become a novelist as well as a poet, and did admire Balzac and, later, *Madame Bovary.* Browning again, in "The Last Ride Together" and, as Baudelaire had just completed the second edition of his volume of verse, George Meredith, in that masterpiece of analytical poetry of love (and of unloving), *Modern Love* (1862), watched that process of love dying in tortured hearts and in too lucid minds, with no recrimination, no insult on either side. The symbolism of the fire dying among the embers, of the awful weight of silence falling over what cannot be conveyed in words is tragic. The inner decay of the illusions of yesterday, the betrayal not from outside but from within are tersely eloquent—more so than in lengthy works of fiction.

> In our old shipwrecked days there was an hour,
> When in the firelight steadily aglow,
> Joined slackly, we beheld the red chasm grow
> Among the clicking coals. Our library bower
> That eve was left to us; and hushed we sat,
> As lovers to whom Time is whispering . . .
> We are betrayed by what is false within . . .

Baudelaire would have been a more complete poet of the dramatic conflicts of sentiment with the relentless analytical power of the intellect if he could have added the gifts of a novelist to those of a poet. Perhaps none of the women whom he loved could render him the service which Proust declares to be the most valuable any loved being can do us: that of making us suffer so as to help us deepen our awareness of ourselves. His life, harried with debts and sordid struggles against family, friends, and a public which did not understand him, did not present him with a partner who might have forced him and herself to apply to each other, as in *Modern Love,*

> that fatal knife,
> Deep questioning, which probes to endless dole.

Nor did he ever secure or seek any feminine friendships: intelligent conversation in a woman drew his contempt as a form of pleasure enjoyed only by pederasts.

As it is, driven by his Catholic sensibility and by contradictions which, unlike a more Olympian genius like that of Goethe, he could never reconcile into a majestic, and selfish, synthesis, Baudelaire left us the most heart-rending picture which French literature has of "l'homme désaccordé," the modern man attuned neither to the world or to others nor to himself. He repeated in his prose works that he saw the human being as a "homo duplex." He was convinced he had been doomed, and damned, from the beginning of Time. But that very disharmony inside himself enabled him to express the plight of the human creature, everlastingly building up illusions around love and forever in need of artists and writers audacious enough to shatter into pieces "ces miroirs déformants de l'amour, où chacun cherche à se puiser," in Jean Cocteau's phrase ("those distorting mirrors of love, in which everyone seeks to draw himself as from a well").

BAUDELAIRE'S FORMULARY OF THE TRUE AESTHETICS

RENÉ GALAND

Whenever critics attempt to define the aesthetics of Baudelaire, they encounter a major obstacle. As Lloyd James Austin points out, it is practically impossible to give a precise meaning to such key words of Baudelaire's terminology as *correspondence, symbol, allegory,* or *emblem.*[1] He might have added a word which appears still more ambiguous, more protean: the word *ideal.* Let me begin by a brief listing of the various meanings this word appears to assume under the pen of Baudelaire. First of all, it may refer to the "splendors lying beyond the

---

[1] L. J. Austin, *L'univers poétique de Baudelaire,* 162–67. The writings of Baudelaire to which I refer are to be found in the following editions: *Œuvres complètes* (Bibliothèque de la Pléiade, Gallimard, 1961); *Curiosités esthétiques, L'Art romantique et autres Œuvres critiques* (Garnier frères, 1962); *Correspondance générale,* Vols. I-VI (Conard, 1947–1953).

grave," to the Platonic realm of perfect Beauty from which the human soul is exiled.[2] On the level of artistic creation, the word *ideal* will then apply to the representation of the visible world, but modified in such a way as to suggest a supernatural dimension beyond material appearances. An essential characteristic of romantic art, according to Baudelaire, is this "aspiration toward the infinite."[3] Baudelaire also gives the word a more general meaning: *ideal* may refer to the representation of reality by the artist when this representation, instead of mirroring nature with photographic fidelity, shows nature modified according to the inner demands of the artist. There are, of course, many ways in which the artist can modify nature when he represents it in his work.

For some artists, the ideal happens to be in complete identity with the real. Such was the case of the fortunate inhabitants of ancient Greece or Renaissance Italy. Nature there was so beautiful and so generous that artists, having nothing more to wish for, could not imagine anything more beautiful than what they saw.[4] Baudelaire does not ask why, if these men found in nature all they might have desired, they bothered to reproduce it in marble or on canvas. A passage he wrote about Ingres suggests the answer he might have given. When Ingres paints a beautiful young woman, the painting reveals a complete absorption with reality, a total satisfaction with what *is*. Such a painting is as robust and substantial as was love on the sunny shores of pagan Greece.[5] Art thus appears as the enthusiastic homage paid to nature by her grateful sons. Only such artists properly deserve the name of "naturalists." Baudelaire shows only contempt for other so-called naturalists, for whom art is limited to the slavish reproduction of external

[2] *Notes nouvelles sur Edgar Poe*, IV.
[3] *Salon de 1846*, II.
[4] *Ibid.*
[5] *Le Musée classique du Bazar Bonne-Nouvelle.*

reality, however ugly it may be, and who find ultimate artistic perfection in photographic fidelity. This degraded form of naturalism has nothing to do with the naturalistic art of Classical Antiquity or Italian Renaissance. It is but a manifestation, in the realm of art, of that misguided philosophy, positivism. A man who embraces positivism puts on blinders. The nature he claims to worship is but a cheap counterfeit, a miserable copy of the real thing. He may be likened to the photographer who believes that he can portray the majesty of ancient heroes by dressing up some hoodlums off the street in antique garb and grouping them into scenes which, once photographed, are supposed to depict famous events from ancient history.[6]

If positivist naturalism is anathema to Baudelaire, other conceptions of the aesthetic ideal are equally dangerous. The artist must not, for instance, confuse the ideal with this "vague thing, this boring evanescent dream floating around the ceilings of academic studios." [7] The ideal is not the stereotype. This is the mistake made by a whole category of artists who ought to be castigated as severely as the fanatics of positivist naturalism. Baudelaire rails at those painters or writers who would force nature into preconceived patterns, according to preconceived codes. He aims his sharpest arrows at those contemporaries of his who write "tragedies" to be performed at the Comédie Française: for them, writing a tragedy means cutting up cardboard silhouettes which stand for love, hatred, ambition, and so on, and manipulating them with wires so as to make them walk, salute, sit down according to the rules and regulations of some mysterious etiquette. These "tragic" authors have their counterpart in painting. A "tragic" landscape is an arrangement of trees, fountains, tombs and funeral urns modeled on

---

[6] *Salon de 1859*, II, III.
[7] *Salon de 1846*, VII.

the standard "tragic" pattern. No "tragic" shepherd will be caught with any other dog than the regular "tragic" dog.[8] Still worse are those who would compel nature to submit, not to a conventional aesthetic code, but to moral, social, or political values. Their works are arbitrary creations born to illustrate a didactic intention.[9]

Neither should the artist confuse the ideal and geometric stylization. Thus the circle is the ideal curve. But since nature knows no perfect circle, forcing the complexity of nature to assume perfect geometric shapes is an absurdity. This is the accusation Baudelaire launches against Ingres. Excessive stylizing leads him to geometric abstraction. Ingres believes that the irregularity of nature ought to be amended. Baudelaire also recognizes the legitimate right of the artist to select, arrange, and interpret nature.[10] But this process must agree with nature's own design. This is precisely where Ingres fails: he does not attempt to interpret nature's intentions. He imposes upon nature a stylization contrary to her own deeper design and which he borrows from outside sources. Thus a woman painted by Ingres may well show the unnatural combination of slim, perfectly shaped fingers and thick muscular arms for the simple reason that Raphael loved such arms and that Raphael is the supreme law in the realm of academic painting. This is the gist of Baudelaire's indictment: Ingres imposes upon the variety of life despotic improvements borrowed from the repertory of academic models.[11] However,

---

[8] *Salon de 1846*, XV.

[9] *Notes diverses sur L'Art philosophique; Les drames et les romans honnêtes; Notes nouvelles sur Edgar Poe*, IV; *Théophile Gautier*, III; *Correspondance générale*, II, 255.

[10] *Salon de 1846*, IV.

[11] *Exposition universelle de 1855*, II; *Le peintre de la vie moderne*, IV. It ought to be noted that Ingres protested violently against such accusations. He professed to copy nature with slavish fidelity and was most indignant when friends told him that he had idealized his model (Amaury-Duval,

Baudelaire is quick to recognize Ingres' power to render with complete perfection the movement and physiognomy of nature whenever he frees himself from the strictures of the academic code. Some of his portraits are "true portraits, that is the ideal reconstruction of individuals." [12] What Baudelaire means here by the ideal is clearly explained in his *Salon of 1846* (VII, VIII). In his fine portraits of M. Bertin, M. Molé, and Mme d'Haussonville, Ingres has studied his models, he has penetrated their character, he has made visible on his canvas their individual sensibility, their soul, so to speak. Ingres is at his best in those portraits where he has captured the inner being, the intimate poetry of his models. When he fails, his failure is due to an excessive respect for the masters of the past, which causes him to replace the authentic poetry of the living model with a spurious poetry borrowed from the classical bag of tricks. When he succeeds, a portrait by Ingres is not a realistic copy, but a poetic interpretation, an ideal reconstruction of the individual in which the deep intentions of nature have been made clear. If art is a struggle between nature and the artist, the better the artist understands nature's intent, the greater his triumph. Ingres' dessin physiognomique may be considered a perfect example of this type of artistic ideal. There is, however, an aesthetic ideal of a higher type to be found in the paintings of Delacroix.

Ingres may be a great craftsman, but he does not reach to the heights of his art, as does Delacroix. Baudelaire draws a fine distinction between the dessin physiognomique, which requires only talent, and the dessin de création, which is the privilege of genius. [13] It is not Delacroix's purpose to render the physi-

---

L'atelier d'Ingres, Paris, 1924, 60–62. I am indebted to Professor Francis E. Hyslop for bringing this book to my attention).

[12] *Le Musée classique du Bazar Bonne-Nouvelle.*

[13] *Salon de 1846,* IV.

ognomy of nature. Genius, Baudelaire says, neglects external nature to represent another reality, similar to the spirit and the temperament of the artist. When Baudelaire states that "all good poets are realists," he gives the word *realism* a meaning it never had for Champfleury or for Courbet.[14] The realists' slogan: "Copy nature; copy only nature," is given the following interpretation by Baudelaire:

> L'artiste, le vrai artiste, le vrai poète, ne doit peindre que selon qu'il voit et qu'il sent. Il doit être *réellement* fidèle à sa propre nature. Il doit éviter comme la mort d'emprunter les yeux et les sentiments d'un autre homme, si grand qu'il soit; car alors les productions qu'il nous donnerait seraient, relativement à lui, des mensonges, et non des *réalités*.

> The artist, the true artist, the true poet, must paint according to what he sees and feels. He must be truly faithful to his own nature. He must avoid like the plague borrowing the eyes and the feelings of another man, however great that man may be; for his creations would then be lies, not realities. (*Salon de 1859, III*)

The meaning is quite clear: for Baudelaire, a work of art can have no claim to the highest aesthetic value unless it is an authentic manifestation of an individual sensibility. The true creative process originates in the depths of subjectivity, not in external reality. To the doctrinarians for positivist naturalism, Baudelaire opposes this protest of imaginative man:

> Je trouve inutile et fastidieux de représenter ce qui est, parce que rien de ce qui est ne me satisfait. La nature est laide, et je préfère les monstres de ma fantaisie à la trivialité positive.

> I find it useless and boring to represent what exists, since nothing that exists can satisfy me. Nature is ugly, and I

---

[14] *Puisque réalisme il y a.*

prefer the monsters of my fancy to trite reality. (*Salon de 1859*, III)

Baudelaire does not explain what he means by "les monstres de ma fantaisie." They may be figures similar to the monsters of Goya or Brueghel, or to the monstrous creatures which invaded the nightmares of Thomas de Quincey. They might also be the monsters which Baudelaire himself saw in his dreams. On the other hand, we know quite well what he means by the "paysages de fantaisie." They are landscapes which have no real existence except in the imagination of man. They are the expression of "human revery." In such landscapes, human egotism has displaced nature. They satisfy man's need for the marvelous. Baudelaire finds them in the paintings of Rembrandt, Rubens, and Watteau, in some British keepsakes, and in operatic scenery:

> Jardins fabuleux, horizons immenses, cours d'eau plus limpides qu'il n'est naturel, et coulant en dépit des lois de la topographie, rochers gigantesques construits dans des proportions idéales, brumes flottantes comme un rêve.

> Fabulous gardens, faraway horizons, streams more limpid than is natural and flowing against all the laws of topography, gigantic rocks of ideal proportions, mist floating as in a dream. (*Salon de 1846*, XV)

These landscapes have no more reality than theatrical scenery, but they answer the inner need of man far better than the paintings of artists who remain more faithful to external reality. In them, Baudelaire finds "his favorite dreams, artistically expressed and tragically concentrated." [15] These images may be false, but they are far closer to the only truth which counts: that of the human soul. They answer the famous definition which Baudelaire gave of pure art:

[15] *Salon de 1859*, VIII.

Qu'est-ce que l'art pur suivant la conception moderne?
C'est créer une magie suggestive contenant à la fois l'objet
et le sujet, le monde extérieur à l'artiste et l'artiste lui-même.

What is pure art according to modern conceptions? It means
creating a suggestive magic which contains both object and
subject, the world exterior to the artist and the artist himself.
(*L'art philosophique*)

Thus conceived, art appears as a victory over the reality principle, as the triumph of the ego over the external world, as the
magical realization of man's primitive dream of unity, as the
miraculous communion of ego and non-ego.

This train of thought leads to an obvious corollary. In order
that the ego may triumph over positive reality, a preliminary
condition must be met: the ego must exist. What makes the
artist is a personality strong enough to impose its power upon
the outside world. Pure art is the necessary expression of a
temperament, of "something essentially *sui generis,* by the
grace of which the artist is who *he* is, and not somebody else."
(Richard Wagner and *Tannhäuser.*) When Baudelaire writes
that a painting has the fragrance of the ideal, or that all great
art is a spiritual triumph, his words have a very precise meaning: when we are faced with such art, we feel that it bears the
imprint of the artist's soul.[16] The word *ideal* thus becomes
synonymous with other Baudelairian expressions: *pure art,
spiritualism, supernaturalism.* The views they embody are the
logical outcome of beliefs held by Baudelaire as early as 1846.
He then gave this definition of individualism: correctly understood, it means the naive and sincere expression of his
individual temperament by the artist, with the help of all the
means provided by his medium. He who has no individual
temperament is not worthy to paint pictures and ought to do

---

[16] *Le Musée classique du Bazar Bonne-Nouvelle.*

menial work for a painter endowed with temperament.[17] Technical prowess is not enough. What is the use of expert craftsmanship if it is not placed at the service of an original temperament? Thus Baudelaire sets Delacroix above all others because his personality is the strongest and the most original. Delacroix is not satisfied with fulfilling nature's intent, with making visible the inner reality of the model. He goes much further. Baudelaire would apply to Delacroix Heine's celebrated statement: "In der Kunst bin ich Supernaturalist."[18] Delacroix never doubts that in the struggle between nature and the artist, the artist must win. Little does he care that there are no pink horses in the real world if he has the power to make them exist in the world of his art.[19] Baudelaire flatly states that " a good painting, faithful and equal to the dream which gave it birth, must be created like a world" (*Salon de 1859*, IV). Delacroix knows that "the artist's first business is to substitute man for nature and to protest against her" (*Salon de 1846*, XII). The work of art is a world which can and must displace the natural world.

It must be made clear, however, that such acts of protest are not arbitrary. They are not the result of deliberate choice, of the desire to be original at any cost. The artist's protest must be as spontaneous, as authentic, as hunger or passion. When Baudelaire states that "the artist, the true artist, the true poet should paint only according to what he sees and what he feels," he is not just telling the artists or the poets what they should do. He fully realizes that this is not, for true poets or artists, a command to be obeyed—it is a necessity which they cannot escape. The poetry which Delacroix puts into his painting is not deliberately sought after: it comes *in spite of* the artist.

---

[17] *Salon de 1846*, I.
[18] *Salon de 1846*, IV.
[19] *Exposition universelle de 1855*, III.

Like all poetry, it is *fatal.* Here is an expression which often recurs in the critical writings of Baudelaire: the fatality of genius. Ingres is inferior to Delacroix because he lacks the "energetic temperament which constitutes the fatality of genius." [20] The nature of this fatality can best be understood in the light of Baudelaire's pronouncements on creative imagination. In his *Salon of 1859* (IV), Baudelaire gives his "formulary of the true aesthetics":

> Tout l'univers visible n'est qu'un magasin d'images et de signes auxquels l'imagination donnera une place et une valeur relative; c'est une espèce de pature que l'imagination doit digérer et transformer.

> All the visible universe is but a storeroom full of images and signs to which imagination assigns a place and a relative value; it is a kind of food which imagination must digest and transform.

But it must be stressed that this metamorphosis, this creative process of the human imagination, obeys laws of its own. Baudelaire would say that genius operates under the control of its own fatality. Although creative imagination is "the queen of faculties," it is subject to mysterious laws:

> [L'imagination] décompose toute la création, et, avec les matériaux amassés et disposés suivant des règles dont on ne peut trouver l'origine que dans le plus profond de l'âme, elle crée un monde nouveau. . . .

> [Imagination] takes apart the whole created universe, and, with the materials which it then gathers and reorders according to rules which originate in the deepest part of the soul, it creates a new world. . . .[21]

---

[20] *Exposition universelle de 1855,* II.
[21] *Salon de 1859,* III.

These "rules which originate in the deepest part of the soul" and which command the creative process of art are not deliberately chosen by the artist. He may not even be aware of them. In his essay on Wagner, Baudelaire observes that the great artist, the great poet *create* first. Then, and only then, do they begin to look for "the obscure laws according to which they created." Baudelaire may pity those poets whose instinct is their only guide, those artists who have not attempted to elucidate the obscure laws which govern the creative process. In his eyes, they remain "incomplete." Nevertheless, they are artists. Baudelaire never questions the primacy of what he terms "instinct." The great artist and the great poet may become critics, they may endeavor to reason their art, to throw light upon the creative process. This does not mean that their creations are anything but a necessary, a *fatal* product of their deepest individuality. The fact that Wagner wrote books about the philosophy of music does not mean that his works are not natural, genuine products. Here, it seems to me that Baudelaire is expressing something which is basically quite simple. He does not see art as a mimesis, as a speculum mundi. Art is for him the mirror of the soul. Thus Baudelaire was among the first to formulate a view of art which has since been widely accepted. It reappears under different forms in the works of Proust and Malraux, the criticism of René Huyghe or Jean-Pierre Richard.

According to Malraux, art makes manifest "the annexation of forms by an inner scheme which may or may not assume the guise of figures and objects, but of which figures and objects are but the visible expression." [22] A century before Malraux, Baudelaire had recognized that the total output of an artist, a painter, or a writer, makes up a single whole which

[22] A. Malraux, *Les Voix du Silence*, 117.

organizes itself according to a fundamental scheme characteristic of each artist. As early as 1832, Sainte-Beuve had expressed the belief that "in order to penetrate the soul of a poet,
or at least to seize upon his chief concern, we must search his
works for the word or words which recur most often. The
word will betray the obsession." [23] From these lines, Baudelaire extracted a critical method which he applied in his essay
on Banville. He enlarged its scope when he stated that "the
choice of subjects expresses the man." [24] According to Baudelaire, there is nothing accidental in the use of words or the
choice of subjects. As he puts it in his essay on caricature,
"in art, and this is something which has not been sufficiently
noticed, the part played by man's free will is much less important than is generally believed." [25] Delacroix's paintings
offer irrefutable proof:

> Tout, dans son œuvre, n'est que désolation, massacres, in-
> cendies; tout porte témoignage contre l'éternelle et incorri-
> gible barbarie de l'homme. Les villes incendiées et fumantes,
> les victimes égorgées, les femmes violées, les enfants eux-
> mêmes jetés sous les pieds des chevaux ou sous le poignard
> des mères délirantes; tout cet œuvre, dis-je, ressemble à un
> hymne terrible composé en l'honneur de la fatalité et de
> l'irrémédiable douleur.

> Everything in his works is desolation, massacre, conflagra-
> tion; everything bears witness to the eternal and hopeless
> savagery of man. Burnt down cities, bodies with their throats
> cut, raped women, children thrown under the hooves of
> horses or killed by the knives of their insane mothers;
> the whole of his work resembles a terrible hymn to fate or
> to irremediable suffering.[26]

[23] "M. de Sénancour. 1832," in *Portraits contemporains*.
[24] *La Double Vie.*
[25] *Quelques caricaturistes étrangers,* IV.
[26] *L'œuvre et la vie de Delacroix,* V.

Delacroix may have tried to cover up this savagery, or, in Baudelaire's words, he may have attempted to hide the crater of the inner volcano under bunches of artistically arranged flowers. He did not succeed: his work bears the mark of Moloch. In his savagery, Baudelaire finds the essence of Delacroix's genius:

> Il y avait dans Eugène Delacroix beaucoup du *sauvage;* c'était là la plus précieuse partie de son âme, la partie vouée tout entière à la peinture de ses rêves et au culte de son art.

> There was much of the *savage* in Delacroix; it was the most precious part of his soul, the part totally devoted to the re-creation of his dreams and to the cult of his art.[27]

I would interpret this to mean that the creative energy of genius originates in the depths of the wild ego, at the level of our unconscious drives. Delacroix had struggled to acquire the classical virtues of discipline, sobriety, and critical understanding. Baudelaire praises his efforts in this direction, but what he finds truly admirable in Delacroix is "his violence, his sudden strokes, his unruly composition, the magic of colors," in other words, all that the painter owed to the savage in him.[28]

In Poe's work, Baudelaire observes a similar effort to bring irrational forces under the control of the conscious will and the critical reasoning of the artist. In the creative process, the author of *The Poetic Principle* wanted to give a disproportionate share "to science, to work, to intellectual analysis."[29] This may have been only a fruitless attempt on the poet's part to dupe himself, to convince himself that he was the real master of his genius. Baudelaire goes so far as to suggest that Poe's

[27] *Ibid.*
[28] *L'œuvre et la vie de Delacroix*, IV.
[29] *Notes nouvelles sur Edgar Poe*, IV.

drunkenness was but a means intended to place the creative forces of the self at the poet's disposal:

> dans beaucoup de cas, non pas certainement dans tous, l'ivrognerie de Poe était un moyen mnémonique, une méthode de travail, méthode énergique et mortelle, mais appropriée à sa nature passionnée. Le poète avait appris à boire, comme un littérateur soigneux s'exerce à faire des cahiers de notes. Il ne pouvait résister au désir de retrouver les visions merveilleuses ou effrayantes, les conceptions subtiles qu'il avait rencontrées dans une tempête précédente; c'étaient de vieilles connaissances qui l'attiraient impérativement, et, pour renouer avec elles, il prenait le chemin le plus dangereux, mais le plus direct.

> In many cases, although certainly not in all, Poe's drunkenness was a mnemonics, a method of work, an energetic and deadly method, but a method suited to his passionate nature. The poet had learned to drink just as a prudent man of letters practices by filling up notebooks. He could not resist the wish to see again the marvelous and frightening visions or the subtle conceptions he had encountered in a previous storm; they were old acquaintances which beckoned to him imperatively, and in order to see them again, he took the most perilous, but the most direct road.[30]

Baudelaire does not seem to find it paradoxical or ironical that Poe, the theoretician of the will, of method, of calculation, the poet who would deny the name of poet to those who are not in complete command of their memory or their words, the author of *The Raven,* would consider as an obstacle to be suppressed any control of critical reason, of lucid consciousness. Baudelaire sees Poe's drunkenness as a device to which he resorted deliberately, almost calculatingly, whenever he wanted to stimulate the visionary powers of his imagination. Poe's characters are fascinated by the vortex which can carry them away, and these characters, in Baudelaire's opinion, are none

[30] *Edgar Poe, sa vie, ses œuvres*, III.

other than Poe himself.[31] Here, it seems to me that Baudelaire is getting quite close to Freud. What he appears to be saying is that Poe was fascinated by the visions which rose from his unconscious when alcohol weakened the power of his conscious mind to control the unconscious. When Baudelaire relates the nervous disorders of Poe's characters to "an obstinate chastity," to "the repression of his deep sensibility," even his language anticipates that of psychoanalysis.[32] Baudelaire, as many others after him, seems to establish a link between neurosis and the art of a writer such as Poe.

This is probably the main reason why Baudelaire often finds the fatality of genius so frightening. From Thomas de Quincey, Baudelaire has learned that the human mind is a palimpsest:

> Mais les profondes tragédies de l'enfance,—bras d'enfants arrachés à tout jamais du cou de leurs mères, lèvres d'enfants séparées à jamais des baisers de leurs soeurs,—vivent toujours cachées, sous les autres légendes du palimpseste. . . . Tel petit chagrin, telle petite jouissance de l'enfant, démesurément grossis par une exquise sensibilité, deviennent plus tard dans l'homme adulte, même à son insu, le principe d'une œuvre d'art.

> The deep tragedies of childhood—children's arms torn from around their mother's neck, children's lips forever parted from their sisters' kisses—live forever buried under the other legends of the palimpsest. . . . Some small grief, some small pleasure of childhood, enlarged out of all proportion by an exquisite sensibility, will become the principle of a work of art in the grown man, although he may not be aware of it.[33]

[31] *Edgar Poe, sa vie, ses œuvres*, IV.
[32] *Ibid.*
[33] *Un Mangeur d'Opium*, VIII, 1; VI.

À son insu, unbeknownst to him: those are Baudelaire's words, and they are key words. The rules which govern artistic creation, those rules which originate in the deepest part of the soul, do not come under the control of critical consciousness. Baudelaire has pondered the fate of those artists whom the fatality of their genius has carried off to the abyss. He has reflected on the case of Grandville, for whom nature turned into an apocalypse. Grandville's imagination had broken away from the control of lucid consciousness, and he plunged into madness. But at the same time Baudelaire attributes Grandville's value as an artist to his madness, to the loss of lucid consciousness:

> Or c'est par le côté fou de son talent que Grandville est important. Avant de mourir, il appliquait sa volonté, toujours opiniâtre, à noter sous forme plastique la succession des rêves et des cauchemars, avec la précision d'un sténographe qui écrit le discours d'un orateur.

> Grandville is important because of the mad aspect of his talent. Before he died, he obstinately applied his will power to the notation in plastic form of the succession of his dreams and his nightmares, with the precision of a stenographer who takes down the speech of an orator. (*Quelques caricaturistes français*)

Baudelaire feels ill at ease when faced with the example of an artist who systematically cultivated the disorder of his mind in order to explain with his pencil (and these are Baudelaire's own words) "the laws governing the association of ideas." In his celebrated *Lettre du Voyant,* Rimbaud will remember the lesson Baudelaire saw in Grandville's example. Indeed, the very phrases used by Rimbaud sound like borrowings from Baudelaire. Thus Baudelaire detected in Grandville's works the apocalyptic element to which the surrealists, following in Rimbaud's wake, would also be attracted.

In Goya's *Caprichos,* Baudelaire sensed a similar victory of the unconscious over the intellect. Goya's fantastic works, like those of Brueghel, make the spectator dizzy because they give such a frightening demonstration of the victory of madness, of mystery, of the absurd over the rational mind and will power:

> Il y a dans l'idéal baroque que Brueghel paraît avoir poursuivi, beaucoup de rapports avec celui de Grandville, surtout si l'on veut bien examiner les tendances que l'artiste français a manifestées dans les dernières années de sa vie: visions d'un cerveau malade, hallucinations de la fièvre, changements à vue du rêve, associations bizarres d'idées, combinaisons de formes fortuites et hétéroclites.

> In the baroque ideal which Brueghel appears to have pursued, there are many similarities with Grandville's, especially if one is willing to examine the tendencies shown by the French artist during the last years of his life: the visions of a sick mind, the hallucinations brought on by fever, the transformation scenes which occur in dreams, the bizarre associations of ideas, the strange and haphazard combinations of forms. (*Quelques caricaturistes étrangers*)

Speaking of Goya, Baudelaire goes the whole way. He posits as axiomatic that any work of art worthy of the name is to some extent dependent upon the oneiric vision, upon the obsessions which haunt the artist's dreams:

> ... il y a dans les œuvres issues des profondes individualités quelque chose qui ressemble à ces rêves périodiques ou chroniques qui assiègent régulièrement notre sommeil. C'est là ce qui marque le véritable artiste. . . .

> . . . there is in the works created by deep individualities something which resembles those periodic or chronic dreams which regularly recur in our sleep. This is the mark of the true artist. . . . (*Ibid.*)

Art, like dreaming, originates in the deepest recesses of the soul. This is why, as Baudelaire never tires of repeating, art makes manifest what is most intimate in the mind, the invisible, the impalpable, the nerves, the soul. Baudelaire may therefore justifiably say that "any man's sensibility is his genius." [34] This applies to literature as well as to the fine arts. A powerful novelist is a man whose art is the reflection of his primitive sensibility.[35] It is true that Baudelaire tends to extol the part played in artistic creation by critical intelligence, by the conscious mind, and by rational calculation, but I believe Benjamin Fondane was on the right track when he attributed this excessive valuation of rational consciousness to Baudelaire's fear of the fatality which controls genius.[36] Rational consciousness appears as a defense against the revelations which might come from the inner abyss, against the "demons of the night" from whom, as Sainte-Beuve so acutely guessed, Baudelaire wanted to steal their secrets.[37] The hatred which Baudelaire professed for inspiration may well have had deeper motives than his contempt for such "élégiaques" as Lamartine or Musset. Baudelaire was afraid of losing control, of becoming powerless against forces which he could no longer command, of falling prey to that hysteria which he cultivated with sensuous pleasure, but also with terror. As he said, thinking probably of De Quincey, "inspiration always comes when man wants it, but it does not always go when he wants it to go." [38] De Quincey was for Baudelaire the terrifying example of an artist whom drugs have deprived of any control over oneiric powers and whose mind is no longer able to control the visions and the nightmares welling up from the unconscious. At the

[34] *Fusées*, XII.
[35] Introduction to the translation of Poe's *Révélation magnétique*.
[36] B. Fondane, *Baudelaire et l'expérience du gouffre*, 94–107.
[37] Sainte-Beuve, *Correspondance générale*, X, 423.
[38] *Fusées*, XI.

same time, Baudelaire cannot help being fascinated by the visions born of dream, of madness, of drugs. Banville, he says, refused to gaze at the "marshes of blood," at the "abysses of mud" which man carries within himself. But those poets who command Baudelaire's respect are precisely those who "projected splendid, dazzling rays on the latent Lucifer hidden in every human heart." [39] I do not believe I am going too far if I come to the following conclusion: for Baudelaire, the essential foundation of aesthetic value rests on the unconscious. Genius is essentially individual. Authentic art is the external expression of the inner world of the artist: it brings to light the most secret recesses of the human soul.

On the other hand, Baudelaire does not believe that the individuality of genius is such that a work of art will remain completely closed to other men. The obscure laws which govern artistic creation, those laws which originate in the utmost depths of the soul, are universal laws. Baudelaire has expressed his belief in the essential identity of the human mind. For him, the history of an individual mind represents on a smaller scale the history of the universal mind. Baudelaire finds proof in the striking analogies to be found between the mythologies of all parts of the world. In his essay on Wagner, Baudelaire sees a link between myth, religion, and poetry. They are products of the human imagination, of what he calls "the human revery." There is no essential difference between such collective phenomena as myths and legends and products of the individual artistic inspiration. Faced with the mystery of life, man has always sought to penetrate this mystery, and imagination has been the instrument he used. As Baudelaire notes in his essay on Hugo, poetry, for primitive man, was both "the expression of his soul and the repertory of his knowl-

[39] *Théodore de Banville.*

edge." Modern man may have divorced creative imagination from rational thinking, but creative imagination still remains indispensable, even to a scientist. A scientist who has no imagination may know all that has already been discovered, but he will not discover new laws. Imagination alone will lead to new discoveries, because she is "the queen of the true, and the possible is one of the provinces of the true." [40] Some men have retained the primitive "esprit de chercherie," the inquisitorial bent which compels them to search for the mysterious meaning of things. Baudelaire mentions, among others, Diderot, Hoffmann, Goethe, Poe, and Balzac. [41] Special praise goes to Poe for his concern with these "eternally important problems," speculations about the hereafter, about the workings of the human mind, about the eccentrics and the pariahs of sublunary life. [42] Hugo also looks at the world like an Oedipus surrounded by countless Sphinxes. He too asks the eternal questions: how did the primitive unity of Being engender plurality? Can the primitive unity be restored? Is the number of souls limited, or are new ones constantly created? What is the purpose of the planetary worlds? Does the infinity of stars exist to serve the goodness and the justice of God? Such are the questions which have haunted the "human revery" since the beginning of time, the only questions, for Baudelaire, which deserve to occupy the attention of spiritual man. They are beyond the scope of science, but they are the proper concern of "the poet's inquisitive revery." [43]

In Baudelaire's critical writings, we encounter many converging statements: true poets are those who have "an innate understanding of correspondence and universal analogy"; they

---

[40] *Salon de 1859*, III.
[41] Introduction to the translation of Poe's *Révélation magnétique*.
[42] Note on the translation of Poe's *Bérénice*.
[43] *Victor Hugo*, IV.

hold at their disposal "the inexhaustible fund of universal analogy"; imagination is "the power to see the intimate and secret relationships of things, correspondences and analogies"; it has taught man the moral meaning of color, form, sound, and perfume; it has created at the beginning of the world analogy and metaphor.[44] It must thus be obvious that what Baudelaire calls the imagination is what might be named today the symbolic function or, to use a term popularized by Lévi-Strauss, "la pensée sauvage." Primitive thought proceeds by analogy, like aesthetic perception, and the analogies thus perceived may have empirical as well as aesthetic value. When Baudelaire observes that red, orange, pink, or sulfurous tints suggest ideas of joy, of wealth, of glory, of love, of sensuous delight, he anticipates the discoveries of modern psychology according to which orange and red radiations directly affect the hypothalamic region of the brain and stimulate sexual feelings. When he expressed a preference for sinuous or arabesque lines, Baudelaire clearly had experienced the psychological malaise caused by angular, broken lines, by the physical and mental effort the spectator has to accomplish in order to follow their movement. Conversely, as the art historian René Huyghe has demonstrated, the eyes and the mind find a special exhilaration in the process of following lines which organize visual space according to the deep human wish for symmetry and variety. Baudelaire also opened up the way for such studies as Bachelard's. The analogies which he perceived between certain subjective feelings and certain states of matter were not for him the product of purely individual associations. When he saw in certain animals or plants unequivocal representatives of ugliness and evil, Baudelaire was rediscovering for himself the archetypal symbols which seem to be constant in human nature and which

---

[44] *Théophile Gautier*, III; *Victor Hugo*, II; *Notes nouvelles sur Edgar Poe*, III; *Salon de 1859*, III.

studies on the anthropological structures of the imagination have brought to light.[45] The works of Mircéa Eliade and Gilbert Durand, among others, tend to show that the creative imagination obeys similar laws in all of mankind. This does not in any way threaten the individuality of genius. Individual genius is conditioned by a number of influences which vary with each case. Heredity and childhood experiences play an important part, although there are other factors of a less singular nature at work. There is the geographic environment: Baudelaire has not forgotten the traditional opposition between the melancholy, romantic North and the happy, classical South. Artistic sensibility is also conditioned by the historical situation of the artist. Wagner's Venus is not the Venus of classical antiquity. Centuries of Christian influence have driven her underground. The cave to which she has retreated embodies the horror and the fear with which Christian spirituality looks at this symbol of pagan carnality. Attitudes may have changed, but the symbol has not: Venus remains as a "pure idea," as "the absolute ideal of lust." [46] For Baudelaire, there is only one explanation: all true artists create according to the same laws. These are the laws born of the human soul, the laws of universal imagination. This may well be the main reason why Baudelaire's poetry holds such power over the reader. The images he borrows from the visible world have the fascination of the "pure idea," of the great archetypes.

At this point, it may be of some use to give one or two examples. It is significant that Maurice Blanchot, Jean-Paul Sartre, Georges Bataille, and Georges Poulet should all characterize Baudelaire's ultimate purpose as the conquest of

[45] *Salon de 1859*, IV; *Le peintre de la vie moderne*, VII; *Salon de 1845*, II; *Moesta et errabunda*. René Huyghe, *Dialogue avec le visible*, 28, 166–67, 269–79; *L'art et l'âme*, 478–79.

[46] *Richard Wagner et Tannhäuser*, III.

totality.[47] The definition of art which Baudelaire seems to have derived from Schelling, "mettre l'infini dans le fini," may well refer to this archetypal ambition. Baudelaire has experienced blissful moments when this yearning has been fulfilled:

> Dans certains états de l'âme presque surnaturels, la profondeur de la vie se révèle tout entière dans le spectacle, si ordinaire qu'il soit, qu'on a sous les yeux. Il en devient le symbole.

> In some almost supernatural states of the soul, the depth of life is totally revealed in the spectacle which one has before one's eyes, however ordinary it may be. It becomes its symbol. (*Fusées,* XI)

Mircéa Eliade, the historian of religions, finds a similar conception of the symbol in primitive religions. The perception of such symbols constitutes a paradigmatic experience of reality.[48] This, I believe, is the basic cause of the spell cast over Baudelaire by such spectacles as a chandelier, the patterns seen in a kaleidoscope or a phenakistoscope, the motion of a ship or a carriage, smoke rising from a pipe, arabesque lines, a thyrsus, a seascape. I am in complete agreement with Georges Poulet as to the affective meaning of these symbols for Baudelaire: they suggest a reconciliation between the infinite diversity of time and space, and man's need to encompass the totality of time and space in a single unity. All of these spectacles proffer images of Baudelaire's deepest desire. They suggest a structure of Being which would enable the human mind to grasp the whole of Being as a unified entity.[49] To Georges Poulet's masterful analysis I would add only this comment:

[47] M. Blanchot, *La part du feu*, 143–44; J.-P. Sartre, *Baudelaire*, 50; G. Bataille, *La littérature et le mal*, 44–46; G. Poulet, *Études sur le temps humain*, I, 335; *Les métamorphoses du cercle*, 410.

[48] M. Éliade, *Traité d'histoire des religions*, 374–82.

[49] G. Poulet, *Les métamorphoses du cercle*, 407–27.

most of the objects or spectacles which proved so fascinating for Baudelaire remind the reader of symbols frequently encountered in anthropology. The symmetrical structures of a chandelier or the patterns observed in a kaleidoscope or a phenakistoscope are the equivalent of mandalas. The repeated curves of arabesque lines recall the ancient symbols of the eternal return, of victory over time. The thyrsus combines in a single object the ascending lines, the virile power of the phallus or the royal scepter, and the spiral which suggests periodic renewal and feminine fecundity. Thus the thyrsus offers a symbol in which the celebrated coincidentia oppositorum, the reconciliation of opposites, has been achieved. It is an image of totality.

But the moments during which the depth of life thus stands revealed are the exception rather than the rule. Such spectacles may occur at distant intervals only. For Baudelaire, the essential function of art may well be the deliberate creation of such spectacles, in order that the "almost supernatural states of the soul" which they bring about become the artist's permanent condition. Susanne K. Langer has indicated that the fundamental forms used by artists of all times and places create space for the human sensibility, just as music creates time.[50] The ultimate purpose of art for Baudelaire appears to have been just that—to achieve for man the symbolic mastery of space and time.

[50] S. K. Langer, *Feeling and Form*, 45–103.

RIMBAUD'S RELATIONSHIP TO BAUDELAIRE

MARCEL A. RUFF

The term "relationship" used in the above title was chosen for lack of anything more precise and is therefore not altogether exact. By relationship I simply mean that I shall try to determine to what extent Rimbaud may be considered Baudelaire's successor. I believe that this is about all that can be done, and that it would be excessive to accuse Baudelaire of having fathered Rimbaud. On the other hand, the very fact that I am concerned here with Rimbaud's relationship to Baudelaire also means that I shall have to define the limits of this relationship. If Rimbaud is, in fact, in some ways Baudelaire's successor it is nevertheless obvious that there are great differences between the two writers and that Rimbaud turns away from the path that Baudelaire had opened.

In the early poems it must be remembered that the question is not really one of relationship, but rather of an homage—a token, or perhaps tokens—of Rimbaud's admiration; and these tokens can be noted in the first poetic production by Rimbaud that has survived, "Les Etrennes des Orphelins," a poem that obviously is not Rimbaud's masterpiece. The poem was published at the beginning of 1870, in the month of January,[1] when its author was still very young—not more than fifteen years of age. In it Rimbaud shows, consciously or unconsciously, his admiration for several poets, and in particular for Baudelaire, as may be seen in the following lines:

> Et la nouvelle Année à la suite brumeuse,
> Laissant trainer les plis de sa robe neigeuse,
> Sourit avec des pleurs et chante en grelottant.

> And the new year with her sombre train
> Dragging the folds of her snowy robe
> Smiles through her tears and sings as she shivers.

It is difficult not to see in these lines a vague recollection, a reminiscence of the sonnet "Recueillement":[2]

> . . . Vois se pencher les défuntes années
> Sur les balcons du ciel en robes surannées.

> See the dead years in their old-fashioned gowns
> Lean down from the balconies of the sky.

Elsewhere in the same poem the hemistich, " . . . en se frottant les yeux," seems to have been borrowed purely and simply

---

[1] The poem was sent by Rimbaud, then aged 15 years, to *La Revue pour tous* in the fall of 1869 and appeared in the review on January 2, 1870.

[2] "Recueillement," first published in the *Revue européenne,* November 1, 1861, was included in the third (posthumous) edition of *Les Fleurs du Mal.*

from the "Crépuscule du matin" [3] of Baudelaire: "Et le sombre Paris en se frottant les yeux. . . ."

Too much time should not be spent on comparisons such as these, for then it would be necessary to re-read entire passages from both Rimbaud and Baudelaire. However, scattered throughout the work of Rimbaud are numerous lines that prove that he had read widely in Baudelaire and that he was truly impregnated by his work. A few examples will illustrate this point.

A comparison has often been made between the sonnets "Voyelles" and "Correspondances." [4] The comparison—if there is indeed one to be made—also serves to measure the distance that separates the one poet from the other.

In "Enfance I," one of the most beautiful of the "Illuminations," we find this slightly puzzling sentence: "Quel ennui, l'heure du 'cher corps' et 'cher coeur' "—puzzling because Rimbaud has put quotation marks around "cher corps" and "cher coeur." To me it seems that he was using a quotation, one obviously borrowed from Baudelaire's "Le Balcon": [5]

---

[3] Le Crépuscule du matin," first published in *la Semaine théâtrale*, Feburary 1, 1852, appeared in *Spleen et Idéal*, in the first edition of *Les Fleurs du Mal*, and was placed in *Tableaux parisiens* when this part was added in the second edition.

[4] "Voyelles" was probably written in June or July, 1871. The date of "Correspondances" (first published in the 1857 edition) is uncertain. Its theme seems to belong to the general trend of thought of Baudelaire in the period 1848-1852. On the other hand, the *Salon de 1846* includes a quotation from E. T. A. Hoffmann which is evidently the main "source" of Baudelaire's sonnet: "Ce n'est pas seulement en rêve, et dans le léger délire qui précède le sommeil, c'est encore éveillé, lorsque j'entends de la musique, que je trouve une analogie et une réunion intime entre les couleurs, les sons et les parfums. Il me semble que toutes ces choses ont été engendrées par un même rayon de lumière, et qu'elles doivent se réunir dans un merveilleux concert. L'odeur des soucis bruns et rouges produit surtout un effet magique sur ma personne. Elle me fait tomber dans une profonde rêverie, et j'entends alors comme dans le lointain les sons graves et profonds du hautbois."

[5] One of the last poems inspired by Jeanne Duval.

Car à quoi bon chercher tes beautés langoureuses
Ailleurs qu'en ton cher corps et qu'en ton coeur si doux?

For why seek your languorous charms elsewhere
Than in your dear body and in your gentle heart?

Although the second part is not quite the same as in Rimbaud, I believe that the expressions "cher corps" and "cher coeur" are nevertheless allusions to Baudelaire. In this case it is not certain that the allusion is an indication of admiration, since Rimbaud begins the sentence with "quel ennui." In fact, I believe that, without trying to criticize Baudelaire directly, he is repudiating a certain sentimentality that he attributes to him. These comparisons must be kept in mind, however, in order to indicate clearly all the ties that link Rimbaud to Baudelaire. At this point they are no more than expressions of the great admiration Rimbaud felt for the elder poet. Thus far, we have only expressions of admiration, a kind of homage —just as one finds in the "Poèmes Saturniens" of Verlaine expressions of respect for all the poets he admired at that time. In the case of Rimbaud such expressions of respect—not only for Baudelaire but for other poets as well—are not so much imitations as they are slight winks or allusions.

The relationship between Rimbaud and Baudelaire is further revealed in certain aspects of technique. Once again our attention is caught by the poem entitled "Les Etrennes des Orphelins," in which we encounter this line which seems to limp: "Ah quel beau matin que ce matin des étrennes," ("Ah what a beautiful morning is this morning of New Year's gifts"). The line is an alexandrine, that is to say it includes twelve syllables and, according to classical rules, requires a pause, or at least an accent at the sixth syllable.

Since the sixth syllable is the conjunction 'que,' the line, according to Boileau, is badly constructed. I might add that, if from the seventeenth century, poets as different as La Fontaine, Molière, Corneille, and Racine sometimes used a rhythm other than the symmetrical six and six pattern, they never allowed themselves to place at the caesura an unaccented syllable, such as the conjunction 'que,' which cannot be separated from what follows. Is this simply the clumsiness of a very young apprentice-poet like Rimbaud? Obviously such a supposition is possible, although invalidated by later poems where one finds now one, now two lines composed in this abnormal, irregular way. Instead of disappearing as his technique developed, irregular lines multiplied to such an extent that, after May, 1871 (which seems to me to mark a turning point in the thought and work of Rimbaud) as many as six or seven lines of this kind are occasionally found in a single poem.

It is of interest to note that at the end of 1865, Paul Verlaine, a young poet twenty-one years old and completely unknown at the time, published a series of three articles which form an enthusiastic study of Baudelaire—the first important study devoted to the author of *Les Fleurs du Mal* in France.[6] In his essays Verlaine made the following observation: "Baudelaire is, I believe, the first in France who has dared to write lines such as these: '. . . Pour entendre un de ces / concerts riches de cuivres . . . Exaspéré comme un / ivrogne qui voit double.'" ("To hear one of those concerts rich in brass . . . as irritated as a drunkard who sees double.") These are also completely irregular lines since here too the caesura falls on an unaccented syllable that cannot be stressed. Baudelaire wrote not just two lines of this type, but at least fifteen. Consequently, with him, it was clearly a deliberate way of modifying the rhythm of the verse and of producing an unexpected effect on the reader.

[6] These three articles appeared in *l'Art*, November 16, December 1, December 16, 1865.

It is quite probable that Rimbaud did not read these articles, for they appeared in *L'Art* at the end of 1865 and the beginning of 1866 when he was only eleven years of age. Moreover, the essays were not republished, and the journal in which they appeared probably did not reach Charleville. But it is not at all impossible that the young poet noticed these irregularities himself. Verlaine was only twenty-one when he made his observation about Baudelaire, and no one had made it before him. But Verlaine was a poet with a sense of rhythm who noted details which sometimes escape critics.

Moreover, Rimbaud made a similar observation about Verlaine, who in turn had taken Baudelaire as a model. Those who have some acquaintance with Rimbaud's work and correspondence know that in a letter written to his teacher Georges Izambard in 1870,[7] the young boy called attention to the volume entitled *Fêtes Galantes,*[8] a collection of poems which Verlaine had just published. In his letter the sixteen-year-old Rimbaud commented: "They are very strange, very odd, but really delightful. Startling poetic licence at times: for example, 'Et la tigresse épou—vantable d'Hyrcanie' is a line from this volume."

This is indeed a line from *Fêtes Galantes,* an irregular line, even more irregular than those of Baudelaire. Baudelaire at least respected the caesura in a visual sense; in other words, if he used an unaccented syllable such as *que, un,* or *ces,* a visual blank still remained after the syllable. Verlaine, on the other hand, used a long four-syllable word straddling, as it were, the two hemistichs. In this case Rimbaud, so far as I know, is the only person who has noted the irregularity, in spite of the fact that the French are very meticulous and finicky in matters of grammar and versification. To be sure, versification

[7] August 25.
[8] 1869.

has today become completely free, but at a time when free verse did not exist and when the regularity of lines was very closely scrutinized, Rimbaud immediately noticed the difference. Thus we are led to believe that in adopting Baudelaire's irregular, broken line, he knew what he was doing. The fact that he was really following a path opened up by Baudelaire is indicative of something more than admiration, since it meant the adoption of certain poetic principles.

At this point the main subject is reached, the matter of poetics —poetics as it relates, not merely to craft or technique, but to the very function of poetry. In this connection some very important parallels are to be found, but, in each case, even if Rimbaud followed Baudelaire for a short time, he soon took a different direction.

First of all there is the matter of language. Baudelaire used expressions that are especially felicitous. In speaking of "evocative sorcery" and of "suggestive magic," [9] he was attributing a mysterious power to poetic language. One might reply that all poets are sorcerers or magicians. The point is that there is a difference when they are conscious of the fact. It is significant that Baudelaire should have openly avowed and professed this powerful magic of language, even when he was very young. In one of his first critical articles Baudelaire criticized the writer for not having understood the combination of words, "words combined with each other," to use his exact phrase.[10]

[9] "Manier savamment une langue, c'est pratiquer une espèce de sorcellerie évocatoire" (Essay on *Théophile Gautier,* 1859); "De la langue et de l'écriture, prises comme operations magiques, sorcellerie évocatoire" (*Fusées,* XI).

[10] "Il ignore les effets qu'on peut tirer d'un certain nombre de mots, diversement combinés" (Review of *Prométhée délivré,* by L. de Senneville [Louis Ménard], published in *le Corsaire-Satan,* February 3, 1846).

If the time is taken to study the poetic work of Baudelaire and to try to understand what is new and surprising in this poetry by comparison with even the greatest poets who either preceded him or were his contemporaries, it is certain that one cannot flatter oneself with having found his secret. His genius is his secret. Nevertheless, it can be clearly seen that what gives this poetry a particular, unexpected character, is the fact that the poetic element comes from the language more than from versification, rhythm, or rhyme. Baudelaire exploits the poetic power of language, the kind of poetic charge which exists in words, but which remains unknown and buried within them if the user is incapable of drawing it out. All great writers have this power. Baudelaire was not, of course, the first to write in this way, but he is perhaps the first poet to have given this element a place of primary importance in his poetics. His poetry is essentially the poetry of language and of words.

Rimbaud said much the same thing in his famous letter to Demeny of May 15, 1871, known as the "Lettre du Voyant": "Trouvez une langue . . . Cette langue sera de l'âme pour l'âme, résumant tout, parfums, sons, couleurs, de la pensée accrochant la pensée et tirant." ("Find a language . . . This language will be of the soul and for the soul, summing up everything, perfumes, sounds, colors, thought seizing thought and extending it.")

I have emphasized these three words, perfumes, sounds, colors, precisely because they are a direct reference to Baudelaire ("Les parfums, les couleurs et les sons se répondent."). It can be seen that in choosing them Rimbaud was thinking of Baudelaire, and that this is not an arbitrary comparison. Rimbaud, like Baudelaire, understood that the poet has an obligation to construct a poetic language. But these three words, perfumes, sounds, colors, send us back, whether we wish it or not, to the sonnet "Correspondances" from which they are taken.

Up to this point I have made comparisons that may be considered conclusive and it is obvious that, even in the matter of language, Rimbaud and Baudelaire are in essential agreement. However, is the sonnet "Voyelles" an application of the principle of "Correspondances," as is usually claimed? They are not unrelated, and it is even very possible that the latter is actually the point of departure of "Voyelles." But it seems that the two poems have entirely different perspectives. "Correspondances" sets forth a system of synaesthetic experiences based on the correspondences between sensations. But these experiences are only the application, the illustration of the central theme of correspondences, which in itself is a mystical theme. Moreover, Baudelaire himself, in another, much later text, refers to "the mystical reality of correspondence." For him it is indeed something mystical, as may be seen in "Correspondances" which begins in a highly solemn and, as it were, religious manner: "La Nature est un temple . . ." In the second quatrain Baudelaire refers to the theory of unity and of universal analogy, which is likewise a mystical theory. For Baudelaire, then, correspondences are an element of a mystical reality according to which the entire visible world is a reflection of the invisible world. The doctrine is that of Swedenborg with which Baudelaire was familiar, since he tells us that Samuel Cramer, the poet-hero of *La Fanfarlo* (an early work),[11] kept Swedenborg's books on his night table.

I am not saying that Baudelaire was a convert to Swedenborgianism; he simply took an interest in this mystical doctrine. It is quite clear that, for him, all things in the world

---

[11] *La Fanfarlo* was published in the *Bulletin de la Société des gens de lettres* in 1847. It is generally believed that it was written earlier, between 1843 and 1846. It was reprinted in 1869 in *Œuvres Complétes*.

were not only in correspondence with each other, but also in correspondence with another world. Thus there are correspondences between perfumes, colors, and sounds which unite with each other in the invisible universe. Herein lies the profound meaning of the sonnet "Correspondances." There is hardly any need to trace the idea much further to see that there is absolutely none of this mysticism in the sonnet "Voyelles."

Rimbaud was perhaps a "primitive kind of mystic," ("un mystique à l'état sauvage") as Claudell called him,[12] and, like Flaubert, who was also completely lacking in religious convictions, there seems to be a mystical element in his temperament. "Voyelles," however, does not really illustrate the principle of correspondence, for it is rather a game—a game played by a very great virtuoso, but a game or poetic exercise on the suggestive power that certain vowels had for him at the moment when he wrote his poem. I say at the moment when he wrote his poem, for there is nothing to prove that, a year later, he would have assigned the same colors to the vowels. Verlaine is absolutely right in saying that Rimbaud did not attach any metaphysical or scientific importance to "Voyelles." In this game we do not even know whether the shape of the vowels counts as much as their sounds. There are critics who interpret the sonnet in accordance with the shape of the letters or even by arranging the letters in all kinds of directions—horizontally or upside down—in an effort to find analogies between the vowels and the images that they had suggested to Rimbaud. Thus it has been necessary to discuss the question of correspondences, even though in this matter Rimbaud was not a follower of Baudelaire.

[12] In his Preface to Rimbaud's Works, Mercure de France edition, 1912.

Another factor must be considered in the matter of Rimbaud's relationship to Baudelaire, the question of *modernity*. Beginning with the *Salon of 1845* Baudelaire encouraged artists to express "the heroism of modern life," and in the *Salon of 1846* he included a whole chapter on the subject, "The Heroism of Modern Life." In his last major study, *Le Peintre de la vie moderne*,[13] inspired by the painter and draftsman Constantin Guys, he also devoted an entire chapter to modernity. Indeed, he has often been credited with the invention of the term. Baudelaire, who strongly believed that art should be modern, adopted it and gave it its true character.

Rimbaud also was concerned with modernity, as is evident in the sentence "one must be completely modern," found in "Une Saison en Enfer." Although the comparison with Baudelaire seems striking and almost conclusive, here also one must note limits in their relationship. If the matter is more closely examined it is discovered that for Baudelaire "modernity" comes under the heading of aesthetics: "modernity is the transitory, the fugitive, the contingent, the half of art, of which the other half is the eternal and the immutable."

If, on the other hand, an attempt is made to understand what Rimbaud meant by modernity—especially in his two letters of May 13 and 15, 1871, both of which are known as the "Lettres du Voyant"—it is found that he defined the role of the poet as follows:

> Le poète définirait la quantité d'inconnu s'éveillant en son temps dans l'âme universelle: il donnerait plus que la formule de sa pensée, que l'annotation *de sa marche au Progrès!* Enormité devenant norme, absorbée par tous, il serait vraiment *un multiplicateur de progrès!* Cet avenir sera ma-

---

[13] *Le Peintre de la vie moderne* was written from November 1859 to February 1860 (See *l'Art romantique*, Conard edition, p. 453) and was published in *le Figaro*, November 26, November 28, and Decmeber 3, 1863.

térialiste. . . . L'art éternel aurait ses fonctions, comme les poètes sont citoyens. La Poésie ne rhythmera plus l'action; elle *sera en avant.*

The poet would define the amount of the unknown that comes to light in the universal soul of his own time: he would contribute more than the expression of his own thought, more than the record *of his own steps toward progress!* An extraordinary being becoming ordinary, assimilated by everyone, he would truly be *a multiplier of progress!* Our future will be materialistic. . . . Just as poets are citizens, so inevitably eternal art would have its functions. Poetry will no longer interpret action in rhyme; it will be *in the vanguard.*

It is thus that Rimbaud speaks when he says that it is necessary to be modern. It is true that "Une Saison en Enfer" does not coincide exactly with the "Lettres du Voyant"—far from it. However, on this point, I do not believe that there is any inconsistency in his thought. "Being Modern" is for him being a "multiplier of progress," being "in the vanguard."

During the period 1848–1852, Baudelaire was politically active. It was a period filled with political events: the two revolutions of 1848, the establishment of the Second Republic, and the coup d'état of Napoleon III. During these years Baudelaire was a militant who fought in the streets both in February and in June, 1848 and again in December, 1851, at the time of the coup. He was first a revolutionary, then a republican, and finally an anti-Bonapartist. Baudelaire's political activity modified somewhat his attitude about art and poetry and he came to believe that the artist and the poet should *incarnate* ("every true poet should be an incarnation") and express the ideas of his time, even if form were to suffer slightly as a result.

Within this short period, therefore, it may be said that Baudelaire was not very far away from Rimbaud. However, this was only a passing phase in Baudelaire's thought and after the coup d'état he declared himself "depoliticized."

Not only did Baudelaire abandon politics, but he fell back on art, encouraged perhaps by his reading of Edgar Allan Poe, whose poems and theoretical writings he came to know only in 1852, as William T. Bandy has proved.[14] Much could be said about Poe's sincerity in his essay, "The Philosophy of Composition," which Baudelaire translated under the title, "Genèse d'un poème." For his part Baudelaire was surely not deceived. Despite this fact, however, it is certain that at this period he returned to his original conviction that poetry and art should under no circumstances explain, instruct, or expound anything whatever: neither politics, nor, of course, morality, nor philosophy, nor even passion. All of these should be excluded from poetry. Consequently, he is completely different from Rimbaud both on this point and on the question of progress itself.

Baudelaire wrote some violent passages against the idea of progress—not against material progress which can be of practical value, but against the idea that material or industrial progress is true progress. "There can be no true progress," he wrote, "that is to say moral progress, except in the individual and through the individual himself."[15] That is his position. The modernity in which he continued to be interested for aesthetic reasons is therefore not at all the same as that of Rimbaud.

---

[14] "New Light on Baudelaire and Poe," in *Yale French Studies*, No. 10, pp. 65–69.

[15] This quotation is taken from *Mon Coeur mis à nu*, IX, but Baudelaire has written on the subject on different occasions, notably in *Exposition universelle de 1855*, I, and *Salon de 1859*, II.

Baudelaire's conception of modernity is also connected with the question of Nature. His attitude toward nature has often been badly presented, in particular by Jean-Paul Sartre who claims that nature bored Baudelaire. Not at all! The question is much more complex and profound. Baudelaire was as sensitive to nature as any other poet and he has proved it a hundred times in his work. But in Baudelaire's judgment nature in itself was not a subject for the artist. Nature may be used and should be used by the artist, but only in relation to man: "Any landscape painter who does not know how to translate a feeling by means of an assemblage of vegetable or mineral matter is not an artist." [16] It should be noted that this was not Amiel's formula: "A landscape is a state of the soul." For Baudelaire, it is the reverse: it is the soul that is a land-scape. "Vous êtes un beau ciel d'automne clair et rose" (You are a beautiful autumn sky, serene and rose) he will say to a woman, but he will not say to the autumn sky that it makes him think of a woman. With him, everything is associated with man, with the human being. Even when he evokes nature, his term of comparison is very often something human. Where most writers and poets would tend to say that a cathedral evokes the image of a forest, Baudelaire writes: "Great forests, you frighten me as do cathedrals."

Now with Rimbaud one often has the impression that he is doing something similar. Rimbaud's poem entitled "Ce qu'on dit au poète à propos de fleurs" was recently (1925) discovered in a letter to Banville. It has been interpreted in many ways. In it Rimbaud seems to be mocking poets who talk too much about flowers and who do so from a strictly poetic point of view:

[16] "Le Paysage," in *Salon de 1859*, VII.

De tes noirs Poèmes,—Jongleur!
Blancs, verts et rouges dioptriques,
Que s'évadent d'étranges fleurs
Et des papillons électriques!

Voilà! c'est le Siècle d'enfer!
Et les poteaux télégraphiques
Vont orner,—lyre aux chants de fer
Tes omoplates magnifiques!

Surtout, rime une version
Sur le mal des pommes de terre!
—Et, pour la composition
De Poèmes pleins de mystère

Qu'on doive lire de Tréguier
A Paramaribo rachète
Des Tomes de Monsieur Figuier,
—Illustrés—chez Monsieur Hachette!

Let strange flowers and electric butterflies escape, o
jongleur! from your poems—black, white, green and
dioptric red!
Behold! this is the Century of hell! And the tele-
graph poles, a lyre singing songs of iron, will adorn
your magnificent shoulder blades!
Above all, compose verses on the potato blight—and,
as for the composition of Poems full of mystery
To be read from Tréguier to Paramaribo, buy some
Tomes by Monsieur Figuier—illustrated!—at Hachette's!

Rimbaud invites the poet to document himself, to study
something, even botany, before writing poems about flowers.
His ironic attitude is analogous to Baudelaire's equally ironic
attitude toward nature lovers. In an anthology entitled *Fontainebleau,* published in 1855,[17] Baudelaire contributed two

---

[17] *Hommage à C. F. Denecourt—Fontainebleau—Paysages—Légendes—
Fantaisies.* Hachette, 1855. Denecourt, who had fought under Napoléon,

previously published poems, the two "Crépuscules," as well as two prose poems which were the first of his prose poems to appear in print. With his contributions Baudelaire added a letter addressed to a friend named Desnoyers, and intended as a prefatory note:

> Mon cher Desnoyers,
> Vous me demandez des vers pour votre petit volume, des vers sur la *Nature,* n'est-ce pas? sur les bois, les grands chênes, la verdure, les insectes,—le soleil sans doute? Mais, vous savez bien que je suis incapable de m'attendrir sur les végétaux et que mon âme est rebelle à cette singulière religion nouvelle, qui aura toujours, ce me semble, pour tout être *spirituel* je ne sais quoi de *shocking.*

> My dear Desnoyers:
> You ask me for some verses for your little anthology, verses about *Nature,* I believe, about forests, great oaks, verdure, insects—and perhaps even the sun? But you know perfectly well that I can't become sentimental about vegetation and that my soul rebels against that strange new religion which to my mind will always have something *shocking* about it for every *spiritual* person.

Although we must remember one of Baudelaire's habits, his sarcastic way of expressing himself, he is obviously saying exactly what he thinks.

Outwardly, Baudelaire's ideas of nature poetry are not very different from those of Rimbaud, yet here again it is necessary to note an important difference. If Baudelaire rejects nature by itself as a theme for the artist, if he even rejects pure

---

retired in the Forest of Fontainebleau and spent all his time and savings in an endeavor to improve the place. As the forest was much visited by artists and writers, they decided to publish the book as a token of gratitude towards Denecourt. Baudelaire's contribution included the two "Crépuscules" (which are part of "Tableaux parisiens" in *Les Fleurs du Mal*) and "le Crépuscule du Soir" and "la Solitude," the first prose poems of his to be published (cf. *Petits Poèmes en prose,* XXIII & XXIV). The letter to Desnoyers was printed as an introduction to Baudelaire's contribution.

landscape for the painter, it is for spiritual reasons, as he indicates in the phrase: "for every *spiritual* person . . ." What counts for the poet and artist in Baudelaire's eyes is man and the destiny of man. Nature is important only because it is associated with man's destiny; but if man is detached from nature, then the latter is no longer worth being interpreted by the writer.

With Rimbaud there is nothing of this kind. When Baudelaire wished to disassociate himself from Realism, he made some notes for an article which include the following notation: "Poetry is what is most real, what is completely true only in *another world*." [18] The same reason that prompted Baudelaire to reject Realism also explains his rejection of nature as a unique, exclusive theme for art. Nature is too lacking in spirituality. Man alone has a spiritual life, whereas nature is merely an element that envelops the spirituality of man. For Rimbaud the contrary is true: he loved nature directly for itself. One of his first poems, "Sensation" (which has only eight lines), is already a cry of admiration and of feverish enthusiasm for nature. Nature is inseparable from his work. Everything comes back to nature and the life of nature, but without anything beyond. For Rimbaud the other world of which Baudelaire speaks does not exist. Nature is both a source of joy and even a field of action, as he explains in "Ce qu'on dit au poète à propos de fleurs."

---

[18] "La Poésie est ce qu'il y a de plus réel, c'est ce qui n'est complètement vrai que dans *un autre monde.*" That sentence is found in the notes prepared by Baudelaire for an article under the title: Puisque réalisme il y a" (Since Realism there is). As the same words were written by Courbet in a letter to Champfleury, 1855, it is believed that Baudelaire wrote his notes in the same year. The article was never completed.

The crucial point of this discussion is the question of the Seer. In his famous letter of 1871 Rimbaud wrote:

> Les seconds romantiques sont très *voyants:* Théophile Gautier, Leconte de Lisle, Théodore de Banville. Mais inspecter l'invisible et entendre l'inouï étant autre chose que reprendre l'esprit des choses mortes, Baudelaire est le premier voyant, roi des poètes, *un vrai Dieu.*

> The romanticists of the second generation are indeed *seers:* Théophile Gautier, Leconte de Lisle, Théodore de Banville. But since seeing the invisible and hearing the unheard is quite different from recapturing the spirit of things long since dead, Baudelaire is the first of the seers, the king of poets, *a veritable God.*

Clearly these are terms that show great admiration and which at the same time seem to associate Baudelaire with the theory of the Seer. It is quite possible that Rimbaud borrowed part of the theory from Baudelaire himself. In the "Lettre du Voyant" he maintains that the Seer should create for himself a "monstrous soul":

> Il s'agit de faire l'âme monstrueuse: à l'instar des *comprachicos,* quoi! Imaginez un homme s'implantant et se cultivant des verrues sur le visage. . . . Le Poète se fait *voyant* par un long, immense et raisonné *dérèglement de tous les sens.*

> It is a question of having to create a monstrous soul; like the *comprachicos,* you see! Imagine a man implanting and cultivating warts on his face. . . . The Poet makes himself a seer through a long, prodigious and reasoned *derangement of all the senses.*

In the short story *La Fanfarlo,* where Rimbaud must certainly have read it, the poet-hero Samuel Cramer has written a collection of poems entitled *Les Orfraies.* The poems are supposed to be rather frightening, the kind that Baudelaire was reputed to be writing at just that time. One of Cramer's feminine friends, whom he had known from childhood, reproaches him and he replies:

> Madame, plaignez-moi, ou plutôt plaignez-nous, car j'ai beaucoup de frères de ma sorte. . . . Nous nous sommes tellement appliqués à sophistiquer notre coeur, nous avons tant abusé du microscope pour étudier les hideuses excroissances et les honteuses verrues dont il est couvert, et que nous grossissons à plaisir, qu'il est impossible que nous parlions le langage des autres hommes. Ils vivent pour vivre, et nous, hélas! nous vivons pour savoir. Tout le mystère est là.

> Madam, pity me, or rather pity us, for many of my companions have the same disposition. . . . We have worked so hard to develop sophisticated hearts, we have so much abused the microscope in order to study the hideous excrescences and the shameful warts [the same word used by Rimbaud] with which it is covered, and that we magnify at will, that it is impossible for us to speak the language of other men. They live for the sake of living, and we, alas! we live for the sake of knowing. Therein lies the whole mystery.

Thus, Baudelaire, even at that period, also had a theory of the Seer. Although there is an obvious parallelism between the positions of the two poets in this matter, their theories are not necessarily the same. Rimbaud seems to have been aware that he was borrowing an idea from Baudelaire. But where Baudelaire is concerned above all with the aesthetic aspect of the question, Rimbaud is concerned with something very different. Rimbaud gives the poet an infinitely more important role in society. He was certainly more obsessed by political and social questions than is realized, and it seems that his work is illuminated by the political and social events of his time.

One might say also that revolt and malediction are elements shared by Baudelaire and Rimbaud. Baudelaire not only wrote "Bénédiction," a poem of consolation as well as of malediction, but he also wrote to his mother in 1854: "In short, I believe that my life has been damned from the beginning, and that it will be so *forever*." [19] Similarly, Rimbaud in a letter of 1871 wrote: "I am doomed forever and ever." [20] Even the appeal to Satan that is found in Baudelaire is to be noted in Rimbaud: "Respect the supreme fallen angel cast into outer darkness." [21] Here again, however, it is necessary to see the problem as a whole and to remember that, if at times Baudelaire believed himself damned, or feared being damned, if he sometimes called on Satan, at other times he often repented and showed a very different attitude. In the poem "Bénédiction," for example, he addresses God in the following words: "Praise unto you, O God, who give suffering as a divine remedy for our impurities." [22] At moments such as these he was no longer in revolt against evil and even admitted that evil plays a beneficent role and is capable of purifying man.

There is absolutely nothing of this kind in Rimbaud. Rimbaud was exasperated by the human beings around him, that is to say by the state of society; he renounced the society in which he found himself and cursed it. But his appeal to Satan was purely literary and theoretical. In spite of "Nuit de l'Enfer" and "Une Saison en Enfer," he did not believe in

[19] "En somme, je crois que ma vie a été damnée dès le commencement, et qu'elle l'est *pour toujours*" (December 4, 1854).

[20] "Je suis condamné, dès toujours, pour jamais" (April 17, letter to Paul Demeny).

[21] "Respectez le Maudit suprême aux nuits sanglantes," in "L'Homme juste," an untitled and unfinished poem, probably written in the spring of 1871.

[22] "Soyez béni, mon Dieu, qui donnez la souffrance/Comme un divin remède à nos impuretés . . ."

Satan. His was a hell of an entirely different character, purely interior and fictitious. Here again there is a parallel and at the same time a divergence. It can be expressed in the words of the famous witticism: "They are very close to one another; they are separated only by an abyss."

There is a final point of capital importance, at least from the point of view of the history of poetry, which I should like to stress—a point on which Baudelaire and Rimbaud are in complete agreement. For Rimbaud as for Baudelaire, poetry is not an end in itself. Its only value lies in the power that it exerts. It has a function, a role; it is not a mere objet d'art. Poetry is the act of a poet, of an artist, and at the same time it is a power exerted on the reader.

In the last stanza of Baudelaire's "Les Phares":

> Car c'est vraiment, Seigneur, le meilleur témoignage
> Que nous puissions donner de notre dignité
> Que cet ardent sanglot qui roule d'âge en âge
> Et vient mourir au bord de votre éternité!

> For truly, Lord, the finest proofs that we can give of our nobility are these impassioned sobs that resound throughout the ages and die away upon the shore of your Eternity!

For Baudelaire, this is the meaning of art. All the earlier stanzas of the poem evoke the works of the great artists of the past, contradictory works, some of which, as he says in the last stanzas, are expressions of ecstasy or malediction, blasphemies or Te Deums, in other words, expressions of gratitude to God, or revolt against him. But whatever the form may be, the work of art is the testimony of the artist, the testimony of man, before God.

On the other hand, Baudelaire believes that poetry should act upon the reader, that it should change and inspire him. He would have been in complete agreement with those modern writers who believe that the reader collaborates with the author. So it was with Baudelaire. When he speaks of pictures, he tells us that the true picture is that which excites reflections, meditations, in the person who is looking at it.[23]

For Rimbaud, also, poetry is not an end in itself, for he gave it up at the age of nineteen or twenty and never returned. For him, in his dream, poetry was something which should be a "multiplier of progress." And when he discovered that society had not yet reached the point of accepting that kind of poetry, he went away, he withdrew.

For both Rimbaud and Baudelaire poetry is above all—and this is the summit on which they come together—something of capital importance; all modern art and all modern poetry have sprung from this new conception. For them, poetry and art are primarily a means of stirring the depths, a questioning of the human condition.

---

[23] "Il m'arrivera souvent d'apprécier un tableau uniquement par la somme d'idées ou de rêveries qu'il apportera dans mon esprit" (*Exposition universelle de 1855,* I).

[*This article was translated from the French by L. B. Hyslop and F. E. Hyslop.*]

BAUDELAIRE AND MANET: A RE-APPRAISAL

LOIS BOE HYSLOP
and FRANCIS E. HYSLOP

The name of Manet is invariably associated with three literary giants who, save for the genius with which each transformed and revitalized the literature of his day, differ from each other in the most striking fashion. Baudelaire, Zola, Mallarmé—in all three Manet found friendship, understanding, and support.

But it is with the first of these three, with Charles Baudelaire, that Manet seems to show the greatest affinity. In temperament there are marked similarities: a natural refinement and elegance, discriminating taste, sensitivity to beauty, love of music, and a stubborn independence in the face of a hostile and uncomprehending public.[1]

---

[1] "He [Manet] admitted to me that he loved society and that he took a secret pleasure in the scented and luminous refinement of evening parties. He is captivated by his love of bold, vivid colors, no doubt; but there is also,

Each seems to open a new era in his own domain and at the same time each reflects some of the contradictory tendencies that mark the second half of the nineteenth century. In fact, as Paul Valéry has wisely noted:

> Manet . . . représentait assez exactement à Baudelaire le problème de Baudelaire même: c'est-à-dire, l'état critique d'un artiste en proie à plusieurs tentations rivales, et d'ailleurs capable de plusieurs manières admirables d'être soi.[2]

> To Baudelaire . . . Manet represented Baudelaire's own personal problem: namely, the hazardous situation of an artist torn by several competing temptations, yet capable of several admirable ways of being himself.

The diversity of subjects in *Les Fleurs du Mal* is paralleled by the diversity of themes that may be noted in any catalogue of Manet's paintings. As Valéry points out, a poet who wrote "Bénédiction," "Les Tableaux parisiens," "Les Bijoux," and "Le Vin des chiffonniers," and an artist who painted "Le Christ aux anges" and "Olympia," "Lola de Valence" and "Le Buveur d'absinthe" are not without "quelque profonde correspondance."[3]

Yet despite the correspondences that link poet and painter, Baudelaire has been accused of failing to recognize the genius of Manet and of neglecting to write in his defense, as he did in the cases of Delacroix and Constantin Guys.

No one has been more scathing in his attack on Baudelaire that Philippe Rebeyrol who devoted a long article to the subject in *Les Temps Modernes* of October 1949. Chief among

---

deep within him, an innate need of distinction and elegance that I can see in his works." Emile Zola, *Salons,* eds. F. Hemmings and R. Niess (Geneva, 1959), p. 86. Zola's statement recalls Baudelaire's evocation of the *mundi muliebris* in *Les Paradis artificiels.*

[2] Paul Valéry, *Pièces sur l'art* (Paris, 1934), p. 165.

[3] *Ibid.*, pp. 165–67.

his criticisms is the fact that Baudelaire used Constantin Guys rather than Manet as the nucleus of *Le Peintre de la vie moderne*. In Rebeyrol's opinion, Baudelaire's homage to modernity would have been far more significant had he addressed his praise to Manet, whom he calls the genius of the future.

Rebeyrol's accusation fails to take into account certain significant facts. It is true that Baudelaire had met Manet in 1858 and that his essay on Guys was published late in 1863. But it is important to note that the study had been written long before 1863—between November 15, 1859 and February 4, 1860, as we know from Baudelaire's correspondence. In the meantime, the article had passed from one periodical to another. It had been refused by *L'Illustration*, *La Presse*, *Le Constitutionnel*, and *Le Pays*. In fact, the editor of *Le Pays* had kept it in his drawer for two years and still had it in his possession when Baudelaire, in disgust, gave it to *Le Figaro*, where it was finally accepted for publication—almost four years after the date of composition.

Rebeyrol also fails to recognize the fact that in 1859–60 Manet's painting was far removed from Baudelaire's ideas of modernity. For six years, from 1850 to 1856, he had painted under the instruction of Thomas Couture who, despite certain advanced tendencies in technique, still adhered to the traditional principles of academic art as practiced at that time. It is true that even as a student Manet had rebelled against the artificial and the unnatural. Instead of painting the elaborate historical and mythological subjects acceptable to the juries of the Salon, he insisted that "we must accept our own times and paint what we see." [4] Instead of painting the conventional

---

[4] As a young student Manet read the *Salon* of Diderot, who wrote: "When a society's clothes are mean, art should disregard costume." To his friend Antonin Proust Manet remarked: "That is quite stupid; we must accept our own times and paint what we see." See Paul Jamot, *Manet* (Paris, 1932),

nude, he preferred to paint a model clothed in the manner of the day.

Such unorthodox ideas could possibly have been derived from those expressed by Baudelaire in his *Salon de 1846*. They could also have been inspired by the pronouncements of the Realists led by the artist Gustave Courbet and the writer Champfleury, though Manet himself, like Baudelaire and Flaubert, refused to be included among the Realists. But despite his modern ideas, most of Manet's work between 1850 and 1859 consisted of copies of old masters in the Louvre, which he had painted under the supervision of Couture.

The art historian Moreau-Nélaton was puzzled by the strange lack of original works that marks this long period of apprenticeship. He even wondered if Manet may have destroyed some of his early paintings, so few are the works that remain from this span of years. Of the original studies that survive, none is without the taint of academic art that characterized the school of Couture. A portrait of his close friend Antonin Proust, a picture of an old woman in a linen bonnet, a head of Christ, and an unfinished portrait of the abbé Hurel —all done in 1855 or 1856—clearly reveal the influence of his master.

One of the few paintings of this early period which shows somewhat more originality is the "Buveur d'absinthe," which, nevertheless, was rejected by the Salon of 1859. It has often been suggested that the subject was inspired by one of Baudelaire's poems, perhaps "Le Vin de l'assassin," or that it was an attempt to prove his contention that modern dress has a beauty all its own. Manet may even have been thinking of Baudelaire's statement in the *Salon de 1846*:

---

p. 12. This comment echoes Baudelaire's insistence on the artistic necessity of dealing with contemporary life and dress.

> Les grands coloristes savent faire de la couleur avec un habit noir, une cravate blanche et un fond gris.[5]

> Great colorists are able to create color with a black coat, a white cravat, and a grey background.

But even Adolphe Tabarant, who, with Rebeyrol, has been most critical of Baudelaire, admits that, despite its Baudelairean subject and tone, the painting shows obvious traces of Manet's six years of study with Couture:

> C'est ce qu'eut la franchise de lui dire Charles Baudelaire —inspirateur probable du sujet.[6]

> That is what Charles Baudelaire—who probably inspired the subject—was frank enough to tell him.

Tabarant is referring to an incident related by Antonin Proust in his biography of the artist. When, according to Proust, word reached Manet that the "Buveur d'absinthe" had been rejected by the jury, the painter was talking in his studio with Proust and Baudelaire. Indignant at the refusal, he angrily accused Couture of having influenced the jury. Baudelaire's reply revealed his true assessment of the picture: "La conclusion, c'est qu'il faut être soi-même." [7] ("The sum and substance of it all is that one must be oneself.")

The inference, of course, was that Manet had seen his subject not through his own eyes, but through those of the past— those of seventeenth-century Spanish art and of his idol Velasquez in particular.

---

[5] Charles Baudelaire, *Curiosités esthétiques,* ed. J. Crépet (Paris, 1923), p. 199.

All references to Baudelaire's works are to the Crépet-Pichois edition of Baudelaire, published by Conard. The following abbreviations will be used for the volumes cited: *AR, L'Art Romantique; CE, Curiosités esthétiques; CG, Correspondance générale; OP, Œuvres posthumes.*

[6] Adolphi Tabarant, *Manet et ses oeuvres* (Paris, 1947), p. 29.

[7] Antonin Proust, *Edouard Manet* (Paris, 1913), p. 35.

Many years later Moreau-Nélaton corroborated Baudelaire's opinion. After repeating the story first told by Proust, he adds:

> Baudelaire était dans le vrai. Manet avait beau faire et beau dire: son "Buveur d'absinthe" descend en ligne directe de Couture.[8]

> Baudelaire was right. Regardless of what Manet did or said, his "Absinthe Drinker" stems directly from Couture.

Even Zola, one of the most ardent defenders of Manet, has concurred in Baudelaire's judgment:

> Le peintre se cherchait encore; il y a presque une intention mélodramatique dans le suject; puis, je ne trouve pas là ce tempérament simple et exact, puissant et large, que le peintre affirmera plus tard.[9]

> The painter was still seeking his way; there is an almost melodramatic intention in the subject; in addition, I fail to find in it that temperament, simple and precise, ample and powerful, which the painter will later reveal.

To the opinions of Moreau-Nélaton and Zola should be added those of two of Manet's most intimate friends, the critic Théodore Duret and the Symbolist poet Mallarmé, both of whom came to know the artist after Baudelaire's death. Mallarmé, in particular, was a close confidant of the painter and for ten years came to see him in his studio nearly every day. It is interesting to note that both Mallarmé and Duret agree that Manet's early style was marked by his dependence on the past, though Mallarmé is quick to admit that this "first manner," as he calls it, was an important step in the artist's individual style.[10]

---

[8] Etienne Moreau-Nélaton, *Manet raconté par lui-même* (Paris, 1926), I, 27.
[9] Emile Zola, *Salons,* eds. F. Hemmings and R. Niess (Geneva, 1959), p. 94.
[10] Stéphane Mallarmé, "Les Impressionistes et Edouard Manet," *La Nouvelle*

In fairness to Baudelaire, it should also be added that, if he chose Constantin Guys as the subject of his essay, it was not because he overestimated the work of the elder artist as is often maintained. It was rather because the drawings in question furnished a perfect pretext for presenting some of his favorite ideas on modernity. Not that Baudelaire did not sincerely admire Guys. He was perfectly aware of the lightness, the fluent draftsmanship and the elegance of his works.

But, though he recognized the merits of Guys' drawings and praised them warmly, he by no means mistook them for masterpieces of the highest order. To compare his eulogy of Guys with that of Delacroix is to understand the nature of his admiration. Whereas Baudelaire compares Delacroix to Raphael and Veronese, he compares Guys to Devéria and Gavarni whose sketches of contemporary life make them what he calls "historians." Delacroix, he maintains, is "an unrivaled artist without antecedents, without a precedent"; Guys, on the other hand, is a man of "profound merit" who has "performed a task that artists disdain," who "everywhere has sought the transitory, the fleeting beauty of contemporary life," and whose sketches will some day become "valuable records of civilized life.[11]

Should there be any further doubt as to Baudelaire's intention, one has only to read the opening paragraphs of his celebrated essay, where he clearly implies that Constantin Guys belongs to the category of what he calls the "poetae minores," the lesser great whose work nevertheless contains "du bon, du solide, et du délicieux"—hardly expressions of extravagant praise.

If then Baudelaire devoted his study of modernity to Con-

Revue Française (April, 1959), p. 379. A translation of an English article published by Mallarmé in the *Art Monthly Review* in 1876.

[11] *CE*, pp. 251–52 and *AR*, p. 110.

stantin Guys rather than to Manet, it was clearly because Guys, though of secondary importance, had better represented modernity than any other painter of his time.[12] Manet's production in 1859–60, when Baudelaire was writing his article, was both too scanty and too lacking in authentic modern expression to have justified the title of "painter of modern life."

Though Baudelaire had good reason for not devoting *Le Peintre de la vie moderne* to Manet, one wonders why he failed to write an article in his behalf *after* 1859–60. Is it true, as Rebeyrol, Tabarant, and Jean Adhémar would have us believe, that he made little or no effort to defend Manet in later years, even when the artist was being mercilessly ridiculed and attacked?

First of all, it should be noted that Baudelaire wrote very little after 1861. In fact, the greater part of his most original work was produced before 1860, and some of his articles after that date repeat a good deal of what he had previously written in other connections. Moreover, it was not Baudelaire's habit to write about individual pictures. His essays deal either with the official Salons of the period or with an artist's entire work, as in the cases of Delacroix and Guys, both of whom had already attained their full stature and, unlike Manet, were no longer seeking their way. Moreover, his essays on both Delacroix and Guys were to a great extent pretexts for presenting his aesthetic ideas.

It must also be remembered that Baudelaire knew only a small proportion of Manet's work. If Zola in his laudatory

---

[12] Baudelaire has often been criticized for overlooking Daumier as the painter of modern life. From his correspondence it would seem that Baudelaire had written an enthusiastic article on Daumier in 1861 which was rejected by the editor Martinet. In his letter to Martinet, Baudelaire expresses his regret: "Je suis bien désolé qu'un morceau de critique composé dans un système d'absolue admiration pour notre ami Daumier ne puisse pas vous plaire dans sa totalité." Unfortunately, the article (Baudelaire warned Martinet that he had no copy) has been lost. See *CG*, III, 319.

essay on Manet, published in 1867, admits that he had seen only thirty or forty canvases, it stands to reason that Baudelaire must have seen even fewer, when he left France in 1864 and went to Belgium in a last desperate effort to find a publisher for his collected work. Moreover critics often argue—Mallarmé among them—that Manet's work even in the 1860's was still somewhat derivative and that it was only between 1871 and 1882 that he made his enduring contribution to modern art and became the undisputed painter of contemporary life.[13]

It is true that, among the thirty or forty paintings known to Baudelaire, four or five are often cited as indicative of Manet's true genius and well worthy of Baudelaire's critical attention. Rebeyrol and Tabarant both maintain that Baudelaire's failure to praise them publicly is proof of his lack of understanding and appreciation. Again their accusation seems unfounded. Baudelaire's puzzling behavior may be explained in other ways.

The year 1861 was one of triumph for Manet. It was then that the official Salon accepted for the first time two of his paintings: "Le Chanteur espagnol," better known as "Le Guitarrero," and a portrait of the artist's parents. Not only did "Le Guitarrero" receive an honorable mention from the jury—perhaps through the intervention of Delacroix—but it also won the praise of Théophile Gautier in the official government paper, *Le Moniteur Universel*. Although other art journals were less favorable—if not downright hostile—"Le Guitarerro," with its observation of real life and its portrayal

---

[13] In 1867 Manet's friend, the critic Duret, spoke of the painter as "an artist still too incomplete" and then adds: "M. Manet has been painting for too short a time, and he has not yet given the true measure of what he will be able to produce later to enable me to characterize his manner and to define his work here." Théodore Duret, *Les Peintres français en 1867* (Paris, 1867), pp. 109–10.

of the singer's exotic and picturesque costume, quickly won the approval of the general public.

Even more important, it was much admired by a group of young artists, disciples of Courbet, who on several occasions visited Manet's studio and sought to induce him to join their group at the Brasserie des Martyrs. Manet, who like Baudelaire was something of a dandy, felt repelled by the vulgarity and the crude manners of the Bohemian artists. Unable to accept fully the realistic credo of Courbet and preferring to keep his independence, he refused the invitation and soon became the center of a group of artists at the Café Tortoni.

Manet's success in 1861 brought no public response from Baudelaire, as Rebeyrol points out, but for several very good reasons. In the first place, the fact that he did not write a review of the Salon that year gave him less opportunity to extol the accomplishments of his friend. Moreover, it was the poet, rather than the painter, who was in need of moral support in 1861. Whereas Manet was showing every promise of becoming one of the great painters of the nineteenth century, Baudelaire was at a low point in his career. The preceding year (in January of 1860) he had suffered a slight cerebral attack which left him saddened and depressed. Perhaps because of the attack, he had succeeded in publishing very little in 1860: only a few poems in addition to *Les Paradis artificiels,* which the *Revue contemporaine* had already published in the form of two essays during the preceding eighteen months.

The year 1861 proved somewhat more productive for the poet. In addition to publishing the second edition of *Les Fleurs du Mal,* he finally completed and published his essay on Richard Wagner as well as a series of articles on contemporary writers. But otherwise the year proved to be catastrophic in almost every respect. He suffered constantly from severe attacks of neuralgia and from a recurrence of the syphilis that he had contracted in his youth. The selfishness and infidelity of his mistress, the once beautiful Jeanne Duval, made his reconciliation with her impossible. His candidacy for the French Academy, which he announced in a last attempt to gain the recognition which he so desperately wanted —as much for the sake of his mother as for himself—resulted only in frustration and humiliation.

Even had Baudelaire written an article in support of Manet in 1861, it is highly improbable that he would have succeeded in finding a publisher. The two periodicals on which he had depended, the *Revue fantaisiste* and the *Revue européenne*, ceased publication in 1861 and, to make matters worse, the doors of the *Revue des Deux Mondes* and the *Revue contemporaine* were closed to him as a result of his quarrel with the editors. "Je suis sans journal," he wrote sadly to his mother on Christmas Day in 1861. Small wonder that his thoughts turned constantly to suicide and that he found it difficult to concentrate sufficiently to carry out his literary projects.

In 1862 Baudelaire published his first and only formal defense of Manet, in the form of a short review. The artist had been invited to join the Société des Aquafortistes, an organization formed, with the aid of the publisher Cadart, to encourage etching as a form of artistic expression and sponsored by Baudelaire, Alphonse Legros, and Félix Bracquemond. To the first publication of the Society, a portfolio appearing in September 1862 and containing a preface by Théophile Gautier, Manet contributed an etching entitled "Les Gitanos," based on a painting which he later destroyed.

A few days later, on September 14, Baudelaire wrote a review of the portfolio, which he published in *Le Boulevard*, a small newspaper circulating mainly in cafés frequented by artists. In his review Baudelaire briefly mentions the etching by Manet and calls attention to its strong Spanish flavor which prompted him to believe that "Spanish genius has taken refuge in France." Of more interest is the following observation:

> Manet et Legros unissent à un goût décidé pour la réalité, la réalité moderne,—ce qui est déjà un bon symptôme,— cette imagination vive et ample, sensible, audacieuse, sans laquelle, il faut bien le dire, toutes les meilleures facultés ne sont que des serviteurs sans maître, des agents sans gouvernement.[14]

> Manet and Legros join to a pronounced taste for reality, for modern reality—which is already a good sign—that active and ample imagination, both sensitive and bold, without which it must be said even the best talents are only servants without masters, officials without authority.

The comment, brief but highly favorable, is somewhat puzzling and will be discussed later in the paper.

In 1862 Baudelaire also singled out for praise one of Manet's finest early paintings, the portrait of the Spanish dancer, Lola de Valence. Quite appropriately, his admiration was expressed not in prose but in a quatrain that accompanied the picture and that recalls a comment made by him in the *Salon de 1846:* "Le meilleur compte-rendu d'un tableau pourra être un sonnet ou une élégie." [15] ("The best criticism of a picture may well be a sonnet or an elegy.")

In 1863 Baudelaire again failed to defend Manet publicly when the latter exhibited for the first time two of his best known paintings: "La Musique aux Tuileries" and "Le Bain," better known as "Déjeuner sur l'herbe." "La Musique aux Tuileries," completed in 1862, was displayed at Martinet's Gallery, together with several Spanish pictures, in an exhibi-

---

[14] *AR,* pp. 112–13.
[15] *CE,* p. 87. A few years earlier Baudelaire had hoped to compose verses for Meryon's etchings, but the artist had rejected the idea.

tion that opened on March 1. The "Déjeuner sur l'herbe," which had been rejected by the Salon of 1863, was exhibited beginning May 15 in the Salon des Refusés.

In "La Musique aux Tuileries," Manet, for the first time, treated a contemporary subject in a contemporary manner. The English critic John Richardson calls it "the first truly modern picture, at any rate in Baudelaire's sense of the word 'modern.'" He goes on to describe it as "the first record of nineteenth-century bourgeois life that is detached, realistic and seemingly spontaneous while yet being a work of art." [16]

The painting depicts a large crowd of people who have gathered in the Tuileries Gardens to listen to one of the popular bi-weekly concerts (*Fig. 1*). Manet himself, his brother Eugène, Baudelaire, Champfleury, and Gautier are among the men and women who stand or sit under the trees, forming a series of detached silhouettes, a succession of contrasting dark and light spots beneath the rich green of the trees.

Tabarant maintains that Baudelaire and his friends did not like the picture, despite the fact that it showed no trace of the influence of Couture. His explanation of Baudelaire's indifference is somewhat surprising: "Elle venait trop tôt; elle dépassait son temps et n'était point compris." [17] ("It came too soon; it was ahead of its time and was not at all understood.")

Contrary to Tabarant's idea, there is every reason to believe that Baudelaire may have had a great deal to do with the painting, that he may even have suggested the subject and treatment. In fact, in one of his prose poems, "Les Veuves," which is exactly contemporaneous with the picture, the poet describes a scene very similar to that portrayed by the artist. [18]

---

[16] John Richardson, *Manet* (London, 1958), p. 18.

[17] Tabarant, *op. cit.*, p. 38.

[18] ". . . L'orchestre jette à travers la nuit des chants de fête, de triomphe ou de volupté. Les robes traînent en miroitant; les regards se croisent; les oisifs, fatigués de n'avoir rien fait, se dandinent, feignant de déguster indolem-

This was the time when, according to Proust, Baudelaire was the "constant companion" of Manet, whom he accompanied daily to the Tuileries Gardens while the painting was in progress. This was also the time when Baudelaire was seeking a publisher for *Le Peintre de la vie moderne* and when he and Manet must surely have often discussed the ideas presented in the essay. It could very well be that the painter was trying to carry out some of Baudelaire's theories in an effort to portray what the poet and critic had called "the heroism of modern life." The abrupt change in his style from what Nils Sandblad calls his "paraphrases of Rubens and Velasquez" to the "realism of the flâneur" seems to indicate some such attempt on his part.[19]

In *Le Peintre de la vie moderne* Baudelaire had referred not only to the revival of interest in eighteenth-century engravings depicting contemporary social life but also the growing interest in the graphic art of newspapers such as *L'Illustration* and the *Illustrated London News*. In fact, it was Constantin Guys, the subject of his essay, who had transformed popular journalistic art into something more serious and artistic. It is interesting to note that "La Musique aux Tuileries" bears a strong family resemblance to the engravings of two of the eighteenth-century artists whom Baudelaire singles out for mention

---

ment la musique. Ici rien que de riche, d'heureux; rien qui ne respire et n'inspire l'insouciance et le plaisir de se laisser vivre. . . ."

". . . Through the darkness the orchestra sends forth festive, triumphant, or voluptuous songs. Shimmering gowns trail on the ground; glances cross each other; idlers, tired from having done nothing, loll about, indolently pretending to enjoy the music. Here there is nothing but the rich, the happy; nothing which doesn't breathe and inspire nonchalance and the pleasure of taking life easily. . . ."

[19] "The painting is, actually, in content as in style, a realistic chronicle of the times, stamped with the personality of the artist—and the first of its kind in Manet's production." Nils Sandblad, *Manet, Three Studies in Artistic Conception* (Lund, 1954), p. 32. The first chapter of this book is the most comprehensive study that has been made of "La Musique aux Tuileries."

both at the beginning and at the end of his study—Debucourt and Saint-Aubin. It is equally interesting to note that Manet actually owned two of Debucourt's engravings.

An even closer resemblance may be noted between Manet's painting and a wood engraving, entitled "Concerts militaires dans le jardin des Tuileries," which appeared in *L'Illustration* on July 17, 1858. It is quite possible that Baudelaire's enthusiasm for the works in question proved contagious and helped to steer Manet in the same direction.

Even more significant is the fact that "La Musique aux Tuileries" has much in common with the drawings of Constantin Guys. Jean Adhémar has noted the resemblance and suggests that not only the modern subject of the painting but also its gray tonality are reminiscent of Guys. A letter from Manet to Baudelaire, asking if one must always paint in gray, gives added weight to his assumption.[20]

We are in full agreement with Adhémar and would go even one step further. We believe with Nils Sandblad that a wash drawing by Guys, entitled "Aux Champs-Elysées," (*Fig. 2*) was actually one of the principal sources of Manet's painting.[21] In a catalogue of Guys' drawings, published by Bruno Streiff in 1957, the following description accompanies the picture:

> Peinture étonnante, et très "impressionniste" d'une scène de la vie parisienne, à une époque où pourtant aucun des peintres impressionnistes ne s'était encore fait connaître. Ce feuillet nous donne une indication précieuse sur ce qui Baudelaire avait pu voir lorsqu'il écrivit son *Peintre de la vie moderne*.[22]

[20] Jean Adhémar, "Baudelaire, critique d'art," *Revue des Sciences Humaines*, (Jan.–Mar. 1958), p. 118.

[21] See his study of Manet, *op. cit.*, p. 172, note 66. The authors of this paper made this observation independently before having consulted Sandblad.

[22] Bruno Streiff, *Dessins de Constantin Guys* (Lausanne, 1957), p. 78.

> An astonishing and very "impressionist" painting of a Parisian scene, at a time, moreover, when none of the impressionist painters had established himself. This drawing gives us a valuable indication of what Baudelaire had been able to see when he wrote *The Painter of Modern Life.*

Several significant facts point to the relationship between Manet's painting and the drawing of Guys. It is well known that Manet was lacking in inventive imagination in the matter of composition and that in his earlier works he often borrowed his design from an old master, frequently reversing the figures or objects, either to create a novel effect or because he was working from a print. In the case of "La Musique," it would seem that Manet sought help, not from an old master, but from more *recent* sources, not the least of whom was Constantin Guys.

Certainly, the similarities between "Aux Champs-Elysées" and Manet's painting are striking. Except for a horse-drawn carriage at the left and the absence of the children in the foreground, the Guys drawing is analogous in conception to Manet's painting. One interesting difference is Manet's reversal of the two seated women—a change which is entirely consistent with his practice in many of his borrowed compositions.

The theory that "La Musique aux Tuileries" may have been inspired by Guys is made even more plausible by the fact that Manet was a great admirer of the elder artist. Not only did he do an admirable portrait of Guys many years later (ca. 1880), but at the time of his death he is said to have owned at least sixty of his drawings.

What is even more striking is the discovery that Guys' drawing "Aux Champ-Elysées" was actually owned by Charles Baudelaire and that Manet must undoubtedly have seen and admired it with him. It is even quite possible that the poet encouraged Manet to follow the example of Guys and that he urged him to paint a similar subject in oil. Everything leads us to believe therefore that Tabarant was mistaken in interpreting Baudelaire's silence as indifference and that the poet, on the contrary, was vitally interested and deeply involved.

"Le Bain" or "Déjeuner sur l'herbe" (*Fig. 3*), the second important picture exhibited by Manet in 1863, was shown in the Salon des Refusés together with two of his other paintings and three etchings. This special Salon had been authorized by Napoleon III in an effort to quiet the dissatisfaction of outraged artists whose works—more than 4,000 in all—had been rejected by the reactionary and finical jury of the official Salon. The exhibition became a public scandal. Many of the paintings were undeniably crude and incompetent; a few, like those of Manet and Whistler, ran counter to public taste. None, however, aroused so much antipathy as did Manet's "Déjeuner sur l'herbe."

The picture created a veritable sensation and was considered an outrage to good taste and to public morals: a nude woman sitting between two fully clothed men, dressed in the manner of the day; near them a picnic basket which, together with the woman's clothes, forms a stunning still life; in the background another woman wearing a chemise and bending over the water as if to test it.

According to Manet's own admission "Le Déjeuner" was a transposition into modern terms of Giorgione's "Pastoral Concert." What he did not admit, at least publicly, was that he had also arranged the principal figures in the position of the three river gods which he had seen in an engraving after a design by Raphael. Something about the picture—perhaps the attempt to express contemporary life in terms of an outworn tradition—gives it a certain incongruity and was partly responsible for the feeling of shock that it created.[23]

The entire exhibition was ignored by all publications supporting the government. Théophile Gautier made no mention of it in *Le Moniteur* and Maxime du Camp made only a brief reference to it in his review of the official Salon. Of the other critics, Théophile Thoré and Zacharie Astruc spoke most favorably of Manet; the greater number were ruthless in their attack.

Mocked and ridiculed by both a hostile press and public, Manet was deeply hurt and discouraged. Rebeyrol, sharply criticizing Baudelaire for his "extraordinary silence," seems to forget that the poet was publishing little or nothing at this time.[24] Indeed, he had written very little after 1861. Early in January 1862 he had had a frightening experience. In his *Intimate Journals* this moving notation is to be found:

> Maintenant j'ai toujours le vertige, et aujourd'hui 23 janvier 1862, j'ai subi un singulier avertissement, j'ai senti passer sur moi le vent de l'aile de l'imbécillité.[25]

> Now I suffer constantly from vertigo, and today, January 23, 1862, I have experienced a strange warning, I have felt pass over me the breath of the wing of madness.

[23] A comment made by Alain de Leiris about Manet's painting "Christ insulté" applies equally well to the "Déjeuner sur l'herbe." De Leiris maintains that in the "Christ insulté" Manet did not fully succeed in his attempt to reconcile iconographic and compositional conventions of the past with the objective portrayal of contemporaneous facts empirically grasped. See Alain de Leiris, "Manet's 'Christ Scourged' and the Problem of his Religious Paintings," *The Art Bulletin* (June, 1959), p. 198. Our colleague, Professor George Mauner, recently published a new interpretation of the "Déjeuner sur l'herbe" in *Perspectives in Literary Symbolism* (University Park, 1968).

[24] Although some scholars have conjectured that Baudelaire did not see the Salon des Refusés, others have assumed that he must have visited the exhibition. A letter by his friend Fantin-Latour to Whistler, in which Baudelaire's reaction to Whistler's "White Girl" (included in the exhibition) is relayed to England, makes it clear that the poet did see the show. Information furnished by John A. Mahey of the Peale Museum in Baltimore.

[25] *OP*, II, 78.

Although his fears for his sanity proved groundless, Baudelaire was physically, mentally, and emotionally exhausted. He had not succeeded in finding a publisher for his collected art and literary criticism, he was unable to finish the *Petits Poèmes en prose* "because of my nerves," as he wrote his publisher Hetzel, and he suffered from "the insane idea of my literary impotence."[26] It is true, as Rebeyrol points out, that he did publish an obituary article on Delacroix, but it must be remembered that the article in question was a summing up of twenty years of study and reflection. Moreover, Delacroix was a less controversial figure, and there was little danger that Baudelaire would arouse public displeasure by his eulogy of a man whose genius he had long praised.

Even had Baudelaire succeeded in publishing an article in Manet's behalf at this time, he might have done more harm than good. As George Heard Hamilton reminds us: "To a later generation the support and encouragement of Charles Baudelaire would seem invaluable, but in the early 1860's praise from the author of *Les Fleurs du Mal* was suspect in the extreme."[27] The notoriety he had acquired in connection with the publication of his volume of poetry in 1857 had not been forgotten. When in 1862 he wrote the quatrain that accompanied Manet's painting of the Spanish dancer Lola de Valence, the phrase "bijou rose et noir" had been misinterpreted and given an obscene meaning, which Zola took pains to discredit in his article on Manet written several years later.

Moreover, Baudelaire's support of Manet was well known not only in art circles but among the general public as well. Rebeyrol himself admits that the critic Charles Monselet had called Manet "un élève de Goya et de Charles Baudelaire."

---

[26] *CG,* V, 160.
[27] George Heard Hamilton, *Manet and his Critics* (New Haven, 1954), p. 153.

And in a crude satire appearing in *Charivari* on June 15, 1864, Louis Leroy presents Manet, the conquering hero, as a coldly aloof figure, and Baudelaire, his defender, as a raucous poet, so ill-tempered that he does little more than gnash his teeth and make animal noises.

But though Baudelaire did not publicly defend Manet in the press either in 1863 or 1864 he did what was perhaps even more important and beneficial. He intervened whenever possible and sought to influence those who in any way might be helpful to the artist. When two of Manet's paintings were finally accepted by the Salon of 1864, Baudelaire took time, before leaving for Brussels, to write to his friend the Marquis de Chennevières, who was Director of Fine Arts, asking that he give special attention to hanging the works of Manet and Fantin-Latour.[28]

Unfortunately, Manet's two paintings ("Christ aux anges" and "Episode d'un combat de taureaux") did not reveal the artist at his best, and both were greeted with renewed scorn and abuse. Of all the critics, the most appreciative and also the most perspicacious was Théophile Thoré, who wrote a review of the Salon in the *Indépendance belge* for June 15. Thoré rightly called attention to the fact that the life-sized dead toreador lying diagonally across the foreground of the one picture had been "audacieusement copiée (audaciously copied) from a masterpiece in the Pourtalès collection—at that time wrongly attributed to Velasquez—and that the dead Christ in the second picture was more or less an imitation of El Greco.[29]

---

[28] *CG*, VI, 52–3.

[29] Tabarant, *op. cit.*, p. 83. The "Dead Soldier" is now attributed to a seventeenth-century Italian painter. See Gerald Ackerman, "Gérôme and Manet," *Gazette des Beaux-Arts* (September, 1967), pp. 163-76. Ackerman claims that Manet was inspired by Gérôme rather than by the Pourtalès picture.

Baudelaire in alarm quickly wrote to Thoré, whom he had known some years before, to deny the allegation:

> M. Manet, que l'on croit fou et enragé, est simplement un homme très loyal, très simple, faisant tout ce qu'il peut pour être raisonnable, mais malheureusement marqué de romantisme depuis sa naissance.
>
> Le mot *pastiche* n'est pas juste. M. Manet n'a jamais vu de *Goya*, M. Manet n'a jamais vu de *Gréco*, M. Manet n'a jamais vu la galerie Pourtalès. Cela vous paraît incroyable, mais cela est vrai.
>
> Moi-même j'ai admiré avec stupéfaction ces mystérieuses coïncidences.
>
> M. Manet, à l'époque où nous jouissions de ce merveilleux musée espagnol que la stupide république française, dans son respect abusif de la propriété, a rendu aux princes d'Orléans, M. Manet était un enfant et servait à bord d'un navire.
>
> On lui a tant parlé de ses *pastiches* de Goya que maintenant il cherche à voir des Goya.
>
> Il est vrai qu'il a vu des Velasquez, je ne sais où.[30]

> M. Manet, who is considered a fool and a madman, is merely a very honest and a very simple man, doing all he can to be rational, but unfortunately stamped by romanticism since his birth.
>
> The word *pastiche* is not fair. M. Manet has never seen any *Goyas*, M. Manet has never seen any *Grecos*, M. Manet has never seen the Pourtalès collection. This may seem incredible to you, but it is true.
>
> I myself have been amazed by these mysterious coincidences.
>
> At the time when we were enjoying the marvelous Spanish collection which the stupid French Republic in its excessive respect for property returned to the princes of Orléans, M. Manet was a boy and was serving on board ship.
>
> There has been so much talk about his *pastiches* of Goya that now he is trying to see some Goyas.

[30] *CG*, IV, 276–77.

It is true he has seen some works by Velasquez, I don't know where.

After pointing out that Manet's resemblance to Velasquez was as much a coincidence as his own resemblance to Edgar Allan Poe, Baudelaire concludes: "Every time you seek to do Manet a favor, I shall thank you."

Baudelaire's letter to Thoré was in itself a great help to the artist. Quoting from the letter, as he had been told he might do, Thoré wrote a second article for the *Indépendance belge,* entitled "Charles Baudelaire et les coïncidences mystérieuses." Although he continued to insist on the similarity of the dead warrior and the dead toreador, he concluded his discussion by hailing the young artist as a "true painter" who was worth more than "a whole troup of Rome prize winners." [31]

Despite Thoré's generous praise, Manet had acquired the reputation among the general public and in the popular press of deliberately seeking to shock the spectators and of depending too heavily on Spanish artists in matters of composition and technique. Throughout the rest of his life his work was to continue to meet with misunderstanding and condemnation.

The following year, in April 1865, Manet sent two canvases to the Salon: "Olympia" (*Fig. 4*) and the "Christ insulté." Both paintings provoked a storm of abuse from an already antagonistic public. The "Christ insulté" was based not only on Titian's "Christ Crowned with Thorns," found in the Louvre, but also, as Alain de Leiris has recently pointed out, on an engraving after a painting by Van Dyke.[32] If it met with disfavor, it was not because of its compositional borrowings, but rather because of Manet's failure to idealize or to

---

[31] Tabarant, *op. cit.,* p. 85.
[32] ———, de Leiris, *op. cit.,* pp. 198–201.

sentimentalize the subject. Although inferior to much of his work, it hardly deserved the hostility it aroused.

But it was the "Olympia" which, more than any other work of Manet, enraged both public and critics and was considered an unpardonable offense against decency, convention, and even accepted technique. In this work Manet made a deliberate and conscious attempt to paint a contemporary version of Titian's "Venus of Urbino." It is without question a brilliant example of his technical innovations to which, for the first time, he succeeded in giving coherent expression. But to the gaping spectators, Olympia was not the conventional, idealized nude to which they were accustomed—a goddess or a creature belonging to the distant past or to some exotic clime. She was a brazen young girl "resembling many young ladies of your acquaintance," as Zola tauntingly reminded his readers in 1866.[33] In this respect, she is more reminiscent of Goya's "Maja desnuda" of which Manet may well have been thinking.

The picture, as Zola pointed out, is unquestionably contemporary in character: the slight figure of a young girl reclining on a bed, propped against huge pillows; the Negro servant holding a bouquet of dazzling flowers, obviously offered by an unseen admirer; the black cat arching its back, replacing, no doubt, the cozily sleeping dog in the Titian picture. Everything about the painting bespeaks the courtesan—even the name Olympia, which, suggested by Zacharie Astruc, had doubtless been inspired by the name of a rather brazen courtesan in the celebrated play of Dumas fils, *La Dame aux camélias*.

If "Olympia" is more coherent than the "Déjeuner sur l'herbe," it is precisely because of this contemporary character, because Manet has succeeded in completely modernizing the

[33] ———, Zola, *op. cit.,* p. 67.

classic theme and making it his own. Consciously or unconsciously, he avoided the pitfalls to which Baudelaire had called attention in *Le Peintre de la vie moderne:*

> Si un peintre patient et minutieux, mais d'une imagination médiocre, ayant à peindre une courtisane du temps présent, *s'inspire* (c'est le mot consacré) d'une courtisane de Titien ou de Raphaël, il est infiniment probable qu'il fera une oeuvre fausse, ambiguë et obscure. L'étude d'un chef-d'oeuvre de ce temps et de ce genre ne lui enseignera ni l'attitude, ni le regard, ni la grimace, ni l'aspect vital d'une de ces créatures que le dictionnaire de la mode a successivement classées sous les titres grossiers ou badins d'*impures,* de *filles entretenues,* de *lorettes* et de *biches.*[34]

> If a painstaking, scrupulous, but unimaginative artist has to paint a courtesan of today and takes his *inspiration* (to use an accepted expression) from a courtesan by Titian or Raphael, it is more than likely that he will produce a work which is false, ambiguous, and obscure. The study of a masterpiece of that time and type will tell him nothing about the bearing, the glance, the forced smile, or the real life appearance of one of those creatures whom the dictionary of fashion has successively classified under the coarse or facetious titles of *fallen* or *kept women,* women of *easy virtue* and *tarts.*

The glance, the mien, the bearing of Olympia are indeed of her own time. Despite his compositional borrowings, Manet has remained profoundly original. It may be added that in this respect, he shows a curious resemblance to Baudelaire himself who—whatever he may have owed to others (Delacroix, Diderot, or Poe)—always succeeded in forging something new from the old. The painter had come to realize with the poet that "almost all our originality comes from the stamp that *time* imprints upon our feeling." [35]

[34] *AR,* pp. 68–9.
[35] *Ibid.,* p. 69.

If the composition of the picture was borrowed from Titian, the flavor or tone may have been inspired by Baudelaire himself, as critics have often suggested. Wearing only a bracelet, earrings, a black ribbon around her throat, a flower in her hair, and slippers on her feet, Olympia at once brings to mind the woman of Baudelaire's celebrated poem "Les Bijoux":

La très-chère était nue, et, connaissant mon cœur
Elle n'avait gardé que ses bijoux sonores,

My darling was naked, and knowing my heart,
She had kept on only her sonorous jewels,

Diderot once wrote: "a nude woman is not indecent; it is an undressed one who is." The ornaments worn by Olympia, and in particular, the ribbon tied around her throat, help to create an impression of being undressed rather than nude, and it was in part for this very reason that she shocked and horrified the public, much as her counterpart in "Les Bijoux" had done eight years before. But it is not only the ornaments worn by Olympia that remind us of "Les Bijoux." Certain phrases of the poem—"l'air vainqueur," "le buste d'un imberbe," "les yeux fixés sur moi, comme un tigre dompté" ("the triumphant air," "the boyish bosom," "her eyes fixed on me, like a tamed tigress")—seem as true of Olympia as of Baudelaire's courtesan.

One could even say that the slender figure of the young girl reflects Baudelaire's taste for the slender or thin woman, which is echoed throughout his work. Olympia has the same "maigreur élégante" ("elegant thinness") of the woman in "Une Martyre," the same "nonchalance and impudence" of the "coquette maigre" in "Danse macabre." She could even be "la maigre Adeline" of whose lustful kiss the poet writes in "Le Vin du solitaire."

Moreover, in his many discussions on art with Manet,

Baudelaire must surely have expressed his ideas about the use of the nude figure. "La femme maigre est un puits de voluptés ténébreuses" ("the thin woman is a well of mysterious pleasures") he had written in 1846 in "Choix de maximes consolantes sur l'amour." And among his miscellaneous notes can be found the somewhat paradoxical claim: "Il y a dans la maigreur une indécence qui la rend charmante" ("There is in thinness an indecency which makes it charming").[36]

Equally Baudelairean in character are the Negress, holding the bouquet of flowers, and the little black cat glaring in anger or alarm at the intruding spectator. Strangely enough, it was the cat, reminiscent of the cats that prowl through all of Baudelaire's works, that aroused the greatest furor on the part of the public. Given an almost diabolic significance, it provoked either laughter or scorn and inspired the public to rename the picture, "La Vénus au chat."

Critics have often maintained that "Olympia" as well as certain other paintings by Manet were inspired by poems from *Les Fleurs du Mal*. Zola is among those who have protested most strenuously against this relationship:

> Je sais qu'une vive sympathie a rapproché le poète et le peintre, mais je crois pouvoir affirmer que ce dernier n'a jamais fait la sottise, commise par tant d'autres, de vouloir mettre des idées dans sa peinture. . . . S'il assemble plusieurs objets ou plusieurs figures, il est seulement guidé dans son choix par le désir d'obtenir de belles taches, de belles oppositions. Il est ridicule de vouloir faire un rêveur mystique d'un artiste obéissant à un pareil tempérament.[37]

> I know that a marked compatibility has drawn together the poet and painter, but I believe I can say that the

---

[36] *OP*, II, 5 and *OP*, III, 11. A similar statement is to be found in the *Journaux intimes*: "La maigreur est plus nue, plus indécente que la graisse." See *OP*, III, 11.

[37] Zola, *op. cit.*, p. 91.

latter has never been guilty of the stupidity committed by so many others of wanting to put ideas into his painting. . . . If he assembles several objects or figures, he is guided in his choice only by his wish to create beautiful patches of color, beautiful oppositions of tone. It is foolish to try to make a mystical dreamer out of an artist obedient to such a temperament.

Zola notwithstanding, the correspondences between "Olympia" and "Les Bijoux" are too striking to deny. Yet it would be a mistake to consider "Olympia" a mere transcription of "Les Bijoux" or even to conclude that the poem was its principal source. There is little doubt that, by reading Baudelaire's essays and by talking with him about matters of art, Manet must have been encouraged to turn to scenes of modern life and dress. There is little doubt also that his imagination may have been stimulated by *Les Fleurs du Mal* as well as by the prose poems and translations of his friend.

One must not forget, however, that Titian's "Venus of Urbino" also wore a bracelet and that the slight but elegant figure of the young girl represented, as Sandblad points out, the contemporary ideal of attractive womanhood. Nor can one shut out insistent echoes of Goya's "Maja desnuda." Manet's eyes, like those of Baudelaire, were obviously open to everything around him—to the beauty of the past and to that of the present, to absolute beauty and to relative beauty. It was inevitable that his art should reflect the full range of his vision and that the evocative words of his intimate friend and counselor should have been an important part of that vision.

The scandal created by the paintings stunned and bewildered Manet, who turning to his old friend for advice and encouragement wrote to him in Brussels:

Je voudrais bien vous avoir ici. Les injures pleuvent sur moi comme grêle. J'aurais voulu avoir votre jugement sur mes tableaux, car tous ces cris agacent, et il est évident qu'il y a quelqu'un qui se trompe.[38]

I would surely like to have you here. Insults pour down on me like hail. I would have liked to have your opinion of my paintings, for all this outcry gets on my nerves and it is obvious that someone is mistaken.

From Brussels, ill and forgotten, soon to suffer the paralytic stroke from which he never recovered, Baudelaire wrote a blunt letter calculated to give the artist a severe jolt and to arouse his fighting spirit:

Il faut donc que je vous parle encore de vous. Il faut que je m'applique à vous démontrer ce que vous valez. C'est vraiment bête ce que vous exigez. *On se moque de vous;* les *plaisanteries* vous agacent; on ne sait pas vous rendre justice, etc., etc. . . . Croyez-vous que vous soyez le premier homme placé dans ce cas? Avez-vous plus de génie que Chateaubriand et Wagner? On s'est bien moqué d'eux cependant? Ils n'en sont pas morts. Et pour ne pas vous inspirer trop d'orgueil, je vous dirai que ces hommes sont des modèles, chacun dans son genre, et dans un monde très riche et que vous, *vous n'êtes que le premier dans la décrépitude de votre art.* J'espère que vous ne m'en voudrez pas du *sans-façon* avec lequel je vous traite. Vous connaissez mon amitié pour vous.

J'ai voulu avoir l'impression *personnelle* de ce M. Chorner, autant du moins qu'un Belge puisse être considéré comme *une personne.* Je dois dire qu'il a été gentil, et ce qu'il m'a dit s'accorde avec ce que je sais de vous, et ce que quelques gens d'esprit disent de vous: *"Il y a des défauts, des défaillances, un manque d'aplomb, mais il y a un charme irrésistible."* Je sais tout cela; je suis un des premiers qui l'ont compris. Il a ajouté que le tableau représentant la femme nue, avec la négresse, et le chat (est-ce un chat décidément?), était très supérieur au tableau religieux.[39]

---

[38] Tabarant, *op. cit.,* p. 110.
[39] *CG,* V, 95–7.

I must talk to you once again about yourself. I must try to prove to you your own worth. What you ask is really stupid. *People scoff at you,* the *gibes* get on your nerves; you aren't properly appreciated, etc., etc. . . . Do you think you are the first man to find yourself in such a situation? Do you have more genius than Chateaubriand or Wagner? And yet they were certainly scoffed at. They didn't die of it. And so as not to inspire in you too much pride, I will tell you that these men are models, each in his own genre and in a world rich in genius, and that *you are only the first in the decrepitude of your art.* I hope you will not be angry with me for the *unceremonious way* in which I am treating you. You know my friendship for you.

I wanted to have M. Chorner's *personal* impression, if a Belgian may be considered a person. I must say that he has been kind and that what he told me is in accord with what I know of you and with what intelligent people say about you. "He has faults, weaknesses, a lack of assurance, but he has an irresistible charm." I know all that; I was among the first to understand. He added that the picture of the nude, with the Negress and cat (is it really a cat?), was much better than the religious picture.

Baudelaire's reply may seem unnecessarily severe. Yet it evidently served its purpose, for ten years later Manet was to tell his good friend Mallarmé about the incident and to show him "la bonne et terrible lettre" which he had kept all those years.

Baudelaire was obviously greatly disturbed by Manet's discouragement and loss of confidence. Two weeks later he wrote to Champfleury:

> . . . Manet a un fort talent, un talent qui résistera. Mais il a un caractère faible. Il me paraît désolé et étourdi du choc. Ce qui me frappe aussi, c'est la joie de tous les imbéciles le croient perdu . . .[40]

[40] *Ibid.,* V, 102–3.

Manet has great talent, a talent which will stand the test of time. But he has a weak character. He seems to me crushed and stunned by the shock. What strikes me also is the joy of all the idiots who believe he is done for . . .

Baudelaire himself was unable to do more than encourage his friend:

Quant à finir ici *Pauvre Belgique,* j'en suis incapable; je suis affaibli, je suis mort. J'ai une masse de *poëmes en prose* à répandre dans deux ou trois revues. Mais je ne peux plus aller.

As for finishing *Pauvre Belgique,* I am unable to do so; I have lost my strength, I am dead. I have a considerable number of *prose poems* to publish in two or three magazines. But I can't do any more.

His weakness and ill health did not prevent him, however, from writing his old friend Mme Meurice and urging her to talk to Manet:

Quand vous verrez Manet, dites-lui ce que je vous dis, que la petite ou la grande fournaise, que la raillerie, que l'insulte, que l'injustice sont des choses excellentes, et qu'il serait ingrat, s'il ne remerciait l'injustice. Je sais bien qu'il aura quelque peine à comprendre ma théorie; les peintres veulent toujours des succès immédiats; mais, vraiment, Manet a des facultés si brillantes et si légères qu'il serait malheureux qu'il se décourageât. Jamais il ne comblera absolument les lacunes de son tempérament. Mais il a *un tempérament,* c'est l'important; et il n'a pas l'air de se douter que, plus l'injustice augmente, plus la situation s'améliore,—à condition qu'il ne perde pas la tête; vous saurez dire tout cela gaiement, et sans le blesser.[41]

[41] *Ibid.,* V, 99–101.

Figure 1—Edouard Manet, "La Musique aux Tuileries," 1862. Reproduced by courtesy of the Trustees, The National Gallery, London.

Figure 2—Constantin Guys, "Aux Champs-Elysées," ca. 1855. Reproduced by courtesy of the Musée du Petit Palais, Paris. Photo Bulloz.

Figure 3—Edouard Manet, "Le Déjeuner sur l'herbe," 1863. Reproduced by courtesy of the Louvre, Paris. Photo Giraudon.

Figure 4—Edouard Manet, "Olympia," 1863. Reproduced by courtesy of the Louvre, Paris. Photo Giraudon.

When you see Manet, tell him what I tell you: that torments, great or small, raillery, insults, injustice are excellent things, and that he would be an ingrate if he didn't thank injustice. I know very well that he will have trouble in understanding my theory; painters always want immediate triumphs; but, really, Manet has such light and brilliant faculties that it would be unfortunate if he became discouraged. He will never overcome the lacunae in his temperament. But he has *a temperament,* that is the main thing; and he doesn't seem to suspect that the greater the injustice, the more the situation will improve—provided he doesn't lose his head; you will know how to say all this cheerily and without hurting him.

This is the last mention that Baudelaire was to make of Manet in his correspondence. The pathetic letters that remain to us show him desperately lonely, often too ill to leave his room or even his bed, and haunted by the fear that he would never again succeed in publishing any of his works:

De temps en temps, je conclus fort sérieusement que jamais plus je ne pourrai faire imprimer quoi que ce soit de moi, et que jamais plus je ne verrai ma mère et mes amis. Du reste, je ne travaille plus du tout . . . et mon unique préoccupation est de savoir chaque matin si je pourrai dormir la nuit suivante. Je voudrais dormir toujours.[42]

From time to time I decide quite seriously that I shall never again be able to publish anything whatsoever and that I shall never see my mother and my friends again. Besides, I'm not working at all any more . . . and my sole preoccupation each morning is to know whether I'll be able to sleep the next night. I should like to sleep forever.

Under these circumstances, it is impossible to accept Rebeyrol's claim that it was for Baudelaire, rather than for Zola, to have written an extended study of Manet. Baudelaire had

[42] *Ibid.,* V, 174.

obviously done all he could. It was only during the last years of their friendship that Manet began to reveal the full extent of his originality and, by that time, Baudelaire was already too ill, too weak, too preoccupied with his need to find a publisher to help his friend as much as he might have liked.

It can not be denied, however, that despite his admiration for Manet, Baudelaire reveals in his letters certain reservations even about the artist's more recent works. His frank remark that Manet was only the first in the decrepitude of his art is fairly startling at first glance, but viewed in the light of his aesthetic ideas, it becomes quite understandable.

In the *Salon de 1846* and often thereafter, Baudelaire had emphasized the fact that the art of his day had become decadent and anarchic. The great tradition had been lost, he maintained, and the new tradition had not yet been established by the artists of the day. Failing to find the element of relative or particular beauty that belonged to their own age and time, lacking the creative imagination by which art becomes an evocation rather than an imitation, they had settled either for truth and exactitude (in other words realism), or for didacticism (philosophic art) or for technique for the sake of technique.

In still other cases they had simply gone on imitating a past which had lost its validity for them, thus becoming what Baudelaire calls "artistic monkeys" who ceaselessly repeated the same platitudes and clichés. The absurd idea that progress could be transferred into the sphere of the imagination only worsened the situation, according to Baudelaire, and threatened to cause the world to fall "into the *slumber of decrepitude*" (italics added). It becomes clear then that Baudelaire's seemingly harsh statement was only another way of saying that Manet was the best in what the poet considered a period of artistic decadence in France. And Manet, who must surely have often discussed these very ideas with Baudelaire, could hardly have failed to understand.

Even Zola, writing in 1866, was to admit that Manet would have continued to remain "un reflet," had he continued to paint as he had done in such a picture as the "Enfant à l'épée" (1861). Mallarmé, as we have seen, likewise considered Manet's early work as less original and less modern than the later. Today almost all critics are of much the same opinion. Adhémar has gone so far as to say that Baudelaire was right in not devoting a study to Manet in 1866: "On voit maintenant que Manet, malgré son grand talent, n'est pas le premier peintre de la lignée moderne." ("It is clear now that, despite his great talent, Manet is not the first painter of the modern line.")[43]

What were the faults and weaknesses, the lacunae in Manet's temperament to which Baudelaire alludes in his letters? We can only guess. But we can be more sure of arriving at the correct answer if we are aware of the qualities that Baudelaire most admired in the painting of his day.

In the eyes of the poet-critic, the greatest genius of his time was Delacroix. By noting Baudelaire's explanation of that genius, by observing his analysis of its components and then by applying those components to Manet, we can determine to some extent what he considered the artist's chief weaknesses.

Rebeyrol, it should be added, uses this same method to prove that Baudelaire's romantic predilections prevented him from appreciating not only the merits of Manet, but those of modern art in general. Our concern is necessarily restricted to Manet and to Baudelaire's awareness of Manet's strengths and weaknesses. And it is in this respect that a comparison with Delacroix proves helpful.

[43] ———, Adhémar, *op. cit.,* p. 118.

If Baudelaire prized the work of Delacroix above all, it was in part because the latter was a superb technician, because his work perfectly exemplified what the poet lists as "the three chief preoccupations" of the artist: "movement, color, and atmosphere." [44] Modern critics are in complete agreement. "Delacroix was great," says Hamilton, "because he knew how to do almost everything on which greatness depends—to draw, to paint, above all to compose and to color." [45]

But in addition to his mastery of technique—which Baudelaire would never have considered sufficient by itself—Delacroix possessed imagination, "that queen of faculties," the sine qua non of all great art, whatever the medium. It was through this alliance of imagination with technique that Delacroix was able not only to compose but also to do more than give a mere literal translation of reality. To the author of *Les Fleurs du Mal,* for whom great art was necessarily suggestive or evocative, Delacroix, unlike other artists of his day, had succeeded in suggesting "the invisible, the impalpable, the dream, the nerves, the soul."

Lastly, Delacroix's works are imbued with a certain melancholy which, according to Baudelaire, made him "the true painter of the 19th century."

If we apply these criteria to Manet, we come closer to understanding Baudelaire's reservations. As far as technique is concerned, the most obvious difference between Delacroix and Manet is in the matter of movement:

> Delacroix est le seul aujourd'hui dont l'originalité n'ait pas été envahie par le système des lignes droites; ses personnages sont toujours agités, et ses draperies voltigeantes. Au point de vue de Delacroix, la ligne n'est pas . . .[46]

[44] *CE,* p. 110.
[45] George Heard Hamilton, "Is Manet still 'modern?,' " *Art News Annual* (New York, 1966), p. 107.
[46] *CE,* p. 110.

> Delacroix is the only artist today whose originality has
> not been invaded by the tyrannical system of straight lines;
> his figures are always restless and his draperies fluttering.
> From Delacroix's point of view line does not exist. . .

In contrast, Manet's draftsmanship has a tightness that is
very far removed from the writhing fluency of Delacroix.
Manet's biographer, Perruchot, maintains that the artist de-
tested movement. A century earlier Zola had observed ad-
miringly that Manet liked only "les sujets tranquilles" and that
he treated figures as if they were still-lifes.

It is exactly this quality that explains, in part at least, the
strange impassivity that characterizes much of Manet's painting. It is to be seen in the admirable portrait of his parents in
which there is no relationship, either physical or psychological,
between the two figures looking out into space. It is clearly
apparent in the "Déjeuner sur l'herbe" where the nude woman,
oblivious of the gesture of one of her companions, looks away
from him over her shoulder, as if a photographer had called to
her to turn in that direction. Much the same effect is created
in "Olympia" where the girl and even the cat, ignoring both
the maid and the bouquet, stare at us, as if awaiting the click
of the camera. In "La Musique aux Tuileries," where there is
far more activity than usual, the two women in the foreground
give the impression of holding a pose until the artist allows
them to resume their conversation, while Manet and his friend
Balleroy, who are portrayed at the extreme left, stand as if at
attention. Even in paintings such as the "Ballet espagnol" and
"Lola de Valence" the dancers stand in deliberate, almost
stolid poses, completely unlike those of Degas who seem to be
caught in the very rhythm of life itself.

This curious lack of movement, in striking contrast to the
turbulent lines and the dynamic flow of Delacroix, must surely
have been considered a weakness by Baudelaire for whom

movement was one of the prime requisites of great painting. Equally important in his eyes must have been the lack of intense color. Baudelaire could hardly have failed to note the relative neutrality of Manet's early palette as compared with the brilliance and opulence that he so greatly admired in the elder artist.

But these weaknesses in the technical aspects of Manet's art must surely have struck Baudelaire as less important than what John Rewald calls a "curious lack of imagination," which led the artist to borrow subjects and compositional elements from the old masters.[47] We have already noted what has been termed his "compulsive" tendency to fit contemporary subjects into conventional designs—a device which obviously explains Degas' remark that Manet "never did a brushstroke without the masters in mind."

But such borrowing, though a weakness as compared to Delacroix's inventive genius, must have seemed less serious to Baudelaire than Manet's inability to work from imagination. When he was painting the portrait of Zola, Manet admitted that he was unable to invent or to work without a model, and he refused to allow the novelist to drop his pose even for a moment.

Zola's account is borne out by Manet's life-long friend Antonin Proust to whom the artist once confided his inability to work without a model:

> Quand je commence quelque chose, je tremble en pensant que le modèle me fera défaut, que je ne le reverrai plus aussi souvent que je voudrais le revoir. On vient, on pose, puis on s'en va, se disant: "Il finira bien tout seul!" Eh bien non, on ne finit rien tout seul.[48]

[47] John Rewald, *The History of Impressionism* (New York, 1961), pp. 86 and 198.
[48] Proust, *op. cit.*, pp. 90–91.

> When I start something, I tremble at the thought that the model may fail to appear, that I will not see him as often as I would like. They come, pose, then leave, saying: "He will finish all right by himself!" No indeed, one cannot finish anything by himself.

Even as late as 1881, two years before his death, Manet complained of being unable to work without a model. When Mallarmé wrote, asking him to do some drawings to illustrate a translation of Poe, the artist, weakened by illness, replied that he lacked the strength and then added significantly: "Je n'ai pas de modèle, et surtout point d'imagination." ("I don't have a model, and above all I don't have any imagination.")[49]

This inability on Manet's part to work from imagination is in direct opposition to the theory expressed by Baudelaire in *Le Peintre de la vie moderne:* "all good and true draftsmen draw from the image fixed in their minds, and not from nature."[50] He admits that great artists, such as Raphael and Watteau, made admirable sketches from nature, but these, he maintained, were mere notes. For a true artist who has reached the final stage of a work, a model would be more a hindrance than a help. Only by relying on memory and imagination can he escape the hoard of trivial details that besiege his attention and prevent him from establishing a proper hierarchy within his painting. In fact, one of the reasons that Baudelaire ad-

---

[49] See Jamot-Wildenstein, *Manet* (Paris, 1932), I, p. 102. Manet was obviously in complete agreement with Baudelaire in regard to the role of imagination and memory. His advice to young painters recalls Baudelaire's distaste for precise realism and his praise of the imagination: "Très bon, la science; mais pour nous, voyez-vous, l'imagination vaut mieux." ("knowledge is all well and good; but for us, you see, imagination is more important.")

A year before his death, Manet's advice to Jeanniot is again reminiscent of Baudelaire: "Et puis, cultivez votre mémoire; car la nature ne vous donnera jamais que des renseignements." ("And then, cultivate your memory, for nature will never give you anything more than indications.") See Moreau-Nélaton, *Manet*, II, 96.

[50] *AR*, pp. 71–2.

mired both Guys and Daumier was that they usually worked without models, translating the image stored within their memories.

The same lack of imagination that explains Manet's dependence on a model may also explain the impersonality that marks so many of his paintings. Even those pictures whose subjects should appeal to our deepest emotions leave us as unmoved as a still-life. The "Exécution de Maximilien" (1867), despite its tragic subject, is completely devoid of the emotional impact that marks its counterpart, Goya's "Tres de Mayo." [51] The dead bullfighter (1864) is no more tragic than if he had been taking his afternoon siesta. The "Christ insulté" (1865) seems lacking in spiritual and emotional overtones. In each case, Manet has given what Zola calls a literal translation:

> Ne lui demandez rien autre chose qu'une traduction d'une justesse littérale. Il ne saurait ni chanter ni philosopher. Il sait peindre et voilà tout.[52]

> Don't ask him for anything other than a fine literal translation. He doesn't know how to sing or philosophize. He knows how to paint and that's all.

This literal translation, so admired by Zola, is entirely contrary to the ideas of Baudelaire, who in the *Salon de 1859* calls for "the employment of the imagination and the introduction of poetry into all the functions of art." Not the "alien poetry, usually borrowed from the past," as in the case of Ingres, but the poetry that comes from the "soul," which had

---

[51] In contrast to generally accepted opinion, Sandblad has argued that the painting expresses a strongly felt but firmly controlled emotion. See Sandblad, *op. cit.,* pp. 109–158. Anne Coffin Hanson has recently expressed a similar opinion. See *Art Bulletin* (Sept.-Dec. 1966), p. 435.

[52] Zola, *op. cit.,* p. 92.

enabled Delacroix to express "the *wonderful* aspect of things, the infinite within the finite." [53]

In other words, what Baudelaire most admired in painting, as well as in poetry, was its power to suggest or evoke. With such a conception of art, it is truly remarkable that he was able to recognize the enduring qualities of Manet's paintings, despite their "literal translations," so alien to his own temperament. And it is entirely to his credit that he never prostituted his aesthetic beliefs by falsifying his ideas to Manet, even if it meant hurting the pride of one of his most intimate friends.

Rebeyrol would have us believe that the lack of melancholy in Manet's paintings is one of the principal reasons that Baudelaire failed to appreciate and to defend his art. There is no doubt that Baudelaire shows a strong predilection for melancholy and that he considered it one of the characteristics of modern beauty. Yet if lack of "modernity" failed to lessen his admiration for Delacroix, there is no reason to believe that an absence of melancholy prejudiced him against Manet.

Baudelaire's comments about Manet's art, though few in number, pose two rather perplexing questions. First, if Baudelaire's conception of art was more or less romantic in nature, why did he remark to Théophile Thoré that Manet had "unfortunately been stamped with romanticism since birth"? Second, if Baudelaire believed that Manet was lacking in imagination, as we have suggested, why did he maintain in his review of 1862 that Manet and Legros coupled a pronounced taste for reality with an active and ample imagination?

The question of romanticism is easily solved if one remembers that Baudelaire used the term romanticism in two ways, as Marcel Ruff has so aptly pointed out in his classic study

[53]*CE*, pp. 328 and 298.

L'Esprit du mal et l'esthétique baudelairienne. M. Ruff reminds us that Baudelaire distinguished between two romanti-
cisms: the good and the bad, or rather the true, which is the
good, and the false, which is the bad. As proof for his asser-
tion, M. Ruff reminds us that, in an essay written in 1846,
Baudelaire refers to "the false romantic school" and opposes
it to what he calls "the austere filiation of romanticism." [54]

Margaret Gilman in *Baudelaire the Critic* has likewise noted
Baudelaire's tendency after 1846 to use the word romantic in a
derogatory sense. There is every reason to believe then that
Baudelaire's characterization of Manet was only another way
of saying that he too shared in the decadence that marked the
false romantic school; in other words, Manet was "only the
first in the decrepitude of his art."

As for Baudelaire's praise (in 1862) of the imaginative qualities of Manet's art, it is important to note that he was alluding
to works such as the "Ballet espagnol," "Les Gitanos," and
"Lola de Valence" in which the exotic aspects of contemporary
life are portrayed with little reference to the old masters. This
was the time when, owing to the influence of the Empress
Eugénie, all things Spanish were in vogue. Paris was infatu-
ated with Spanish art and culture. There was even talk of
introducing the bullfight into France. Like Degas a few years
later, Manet turned to the theater for inspiration. In the picturesque appearance and costumes of the dancers who were
appearing for a season at the Paris Hippodrome, he found,
as Hamilton points out, "the accents of beauty and especially of
imagination, that quality which Baudelaire prized above all
others." [55]

If Baudelaire was aware of certain lacunae in Manet's tem-

---

[54] Marcel Ruff, *L'Esprit du mal et l'esthétique baudelairienne* (Paris, 1955),
p. 238.

[55] Hamilton, *Manet and his Critics*, p. 32.

perament, he was also conscious of the "irresistible charm" and the "strong talent" which, he predicted, would survive over the years. Moreover, he recognized a quality that is apparent in Manet's work from the very beginning—a quality which redeems even his earliest and most derivative work. "He [Manet] has a temperament," he wrote Mme Meurice, "that's the main thing." Baudelaire was not using an empty phrase. On the contrary, he believed temperament to be a prime requisite of every great painter. As early as 1846 he had written:

> Qui n'a pas de tempérament n'est pas digne de faire des tableaux, et,—comme nous sommes las des imitateurs, et surtout des éclectiques,—doit entrer comme ouvrier au service d'un peintre à tempérament.[56]

> An artist without temperament is not worthy of painting pictures, and, as we are wearied of imitators, and, above all, of eclectics—he would do better to enter the service of a painter of temperament, as a humble workman.

Zola was also struck by what he called the "incisive, trenchant temperament" which reveals itself in Manet's art. "Une œuvre d'art est un coin de la nature vu à travers un tempérament" ("A work of art is a bit of creation seen through a temperament"), he once remarked. Baudelaire had made a similar observation in 1846 when he noted that a beautiful picture is only nature reflected by the artist. For Baudelaire, as for Zola, the temperament through which Manet viewed creation was strong enough to overshadow his faults and to fully justify admiration for an art which, in certain respects, was diametrically opposed to that which he had long extolled.

One final question remains to be answered: did Manet himself feel that he had been slighted by Baudelaire? Did he resent the poet's failure to defend him to the public?

---

[56] *CE*, p. 88.

To judge from Baudelaire's correspondence, there is not the slightest evidence of any disharmony. His references to "cet excellent ami," his concern and his defense of Manet in his letters to Thoré, to Champfleury, to Mme Meurice, and, of course, to Manet himself, all suggest strong admiration and a very warm and sincere affection.

When Manet was under violent attack in 1863, neither the artist nor his family gave any indication that Baudelaire had failed to be of assistance. On the contrary, Manet's mother wrote to invite the poet to dinner and to express her gratitude for his friendship. Baudelaire's reply clearly reveals the warmth of his feeling:

> Je vous suis bien reconnaissant de votre gracieuse invitation. Quant aux sentiments que je puis avoir pour votre fils, vous savez que je n'y ai pas grand mérite; et ce que vous dites à ce sujet est beaucoup trop gracieux; car il me paraît bien difficile de ne pas aimer son caractère autant que ses talents.[57]

> I am very grateful for your gracious invitation. As for my sentiments about your son, you know that I deserve little credit; and what you say about this matter is much too gracious; for it is very hard for me not to like his character as much as his talents.

Moreover, the critic Théodore Duret, in his biography of the artist, reminds us that around 1860 Manet had only Baudelaire "to befriend and support him." The poet, he maintains, always stood ready to encourage him and on every occasion undertook to defend his most criticized works.[58] Since Duret did not know Baudelaire and since he became a close friend of Manet only after the poet's departure for Belgium, it is

[57] *CG,* IV, 155–56.
[58] Théodore Duret, *Histoire de Edouard Manet* (Paris, 1906), p. 27.

obvious that he must have been repeating what he had learned from the lips of Manet himself.

Before the poet left for Brussels it was to Manet he turned for financial assistance, and during his stay in Belgium it was Manet who often acted as his intermediary, whether to keep an eye on Baudelaire's literary agent or to intercede with some editor on his behalf. If it is true that Manet wrote to ask Baudelaire for an article in 1866, as Adhémar claims, it is equally true that Manet must have understood his reasons for not doing so. Moreover, the fact that years later he showed Mallarmé "la bonne et terrible lettre" and that he often spoke to him of his associations with the author of *Les Fleurs du Mal* reflect only good will on the part of the artist.

After the poet suffered a stroke in Belgium and was brought back to Paris to a nursing home, Manet and his wife were among his most assiduous visitors. Mme Manet, an accomplished concert pianist, would often go and play for him his favorite passages from Wagner, and Manet himself was one of the group that used to take Baudelaire to lunch with them in the early days of his illness. Baudelaire, weak and speechless, could only listen and occasionally punctuate their conversation with the only word he could pronounce—*crénom, crénom* (damn it, damn it).

On one occasion when Manet had failed to accompany them, Nadar wrote to the artist:

> Baudelaire vous demande à cor et à cris. Pourquoi n'êtes-vous pas venu avec nous et lui, aujourd'hui? Reparerez-vous cela vendredi prochain? Vous lui avez manqué, et il m'a surpris quand je suis allé le chercher, en me criant à pleine voix du bout du jardin: Manet!! Manet!! Ça a remplacé le crénom.[59]

---

[59] Tabarant, *op. cit.*, p. 132.

> Baudelaire is desperately anxious to see you. Why didn't you come with us and him today? Will you make amends next Friday? He missed you, and when I went to call for him, he surprised me by crying out in a loud voice from the back of the garden: Manet!! Manet!! That took the place of the usual damn it.

Relating the incident in his devastating attack on Baudelaire, Rebeyrol refers to the poet's anguished cry of *Manet, Manet* and seems to imply that he was suffering from a guilty conscience. As told by Nadar, however, the incident has no tragic overtones. It would seem that it was not so much anguish as disappointment that Baudelaire expressed that autumn day in 1866. His cry, we would like to think, expressed all the affection that he felt for the artist and friend with whom he had shared so many of his thoughts and most cherished beliefs.